HOLY CRAP

et-black h
d given her
h leer came
oking

HOLY CRAP

JUDY KENNEDY

Trilogy Christian Publishers A Wholly Owned Subsidary
of Trinity Broadcasting Network 2442 Michelle Drive
Tustin, CA 92780

Rights Department, 2442 Michelle Drive, Tustin, Ca 92780.

First Trilogy Christian Publishing hardcover edition 2018

Manufactured in the United States of America

The stories in this book are true to life and as much as possible, included with
accepted permission of the persons involved.

10 9 8 7 6 5 4 3 2 1

Library of Congress Cataloging-in-Publication Data is available.

ISBN 978-1-64088-181-5 ISBN 978-1-64088-182-2 (ebook)

To my husband,

Robert

You are my best friend.

You carefully hold my heart.

Thanks for believing in me.

To my daughters

Staci & Kali

You have caused me to experience excessive pride,

and extreme joy.

Your love gives my life intensity.

Your life gives my life validity.

You are gifts of grace I don't deserve.

To my daddy,

Nevertheless, I love you, I honor you.

ACKNOWLEDGEMENTS

Whenever you begin to write about specific moments that shaped your life, it is inevitable that people will be involved. Of course, life is lived out in the presence of others. Intentionally or unintentionally, the people around us make us who we are. When I chose to attempt to place my life experience in written form, I chose to include others. For the most part, names have been changed.

Daddy. The heart of a man defines him. I have chosen to love your heart.

Momma. One thing I know, the love of a mother is truly unconditional.

Bubba. Our love is endless. My knight in shining armor. You rescue me.

Staci. Hope to my heartache. My heritage. My life is honored by your life.

Kali. Music to my madness. You are my psalmist. Your life writes me a song.

Zack. My time with you here, will be eclipsed only by eternity.

Michael, Kathy, Kirley, Jimmy and Janice.

We take life as it is given to us. We do with it what we will.

We share a common thread of brokenness and blessing. Together, the good memories overshadow the difficult ones. Surviving is what it is. I choose Life.

CONTENTS

INTRODUCTION

Using the words "holy" and "crap" together are risky at best for book title purposes. However, it caught your eye long enough to stir interest and that's why it works. Obviously, we all utilize unique verbiage in describing our life's trying and difficult circumstances. When I heard myself using these two specific words together in a conversation regarding all I have lived through, I decided to use them for this purpose.

Everyone has a story. Each of us has survived our fair share of "crap." I have chosen to believe that all of the messy stuff I have endured has been strategically and divinely used in my life to fulfill a purpose. I can look back at every adversity and identify where it has been useful for the greater good in my life.

God knows my entire story, from first word to final breath, and yet He assures me, His plans for me are good.

I have come to believe that every day, every action, every mistake, every triumph, and every wound has passed before His eyes! He has authored the itinerary of my life. There is no struggle, disappointment, betrayal, heartache, or challenge that has come my way that He could not use for His purposes!

I have read stories of beauty outlining glorious tales of broken glass turned into diamonds and cracked pots made into beautiful vases. I have read promises of hope restored and happiness found but I could not find myself in those pages. So, here I sit trying to use the correct vernacular to describe what I believe to be an extraordinary tale of restoration and triumph.

It is unbelievable that one person could live through such a vast amount of challenges. I look back through the years and now clearly see that God had His hands smack-dab in the middle of everything. He was working out His purpose out in my life. He didn't make the messes, but He didn't mind getting His hands dirty and pulling me out of the pile!

The life stories on the following pages are true—every tear, every heartache, and every rescue. I was not called to an easy life; I was chosen to live one of purpose. The conversation that required I use the words "holy" and "crap" together was one I enjoyed having with God. He said it's okay. It's was "crap" but He made it "holy."

I have chosen to write out portions of my life on paper for the benefit of others. I understand that what we have to offer the generation behind us is the knowledge or experience we have earned by living through some things. God uses all that we are to accomplish His plan for us. I am what I am because of what I've lived through. His grace has sustained me, but it's up to me to take the mess I call "crap" and make it fertilizer for others.

I have chosen to break each chapter into four separate units. I'm utilizing an acrostic—Circumstance, Reality, Application, and Purpose. The Circumstance is the portion of the stories and events that actually happened. Reality is a page from a personal journal detailing how I perceived things as they were happening. The Application is simply a small portion of statistics and information I have gathered in regard to my experiences. And I have closed each chapter with a description of how God has chosen to use every season of my life to bring to pass His Purpose for me.

So, let's get started. Keep your heart open, and beware, you may begin to see portions of your life revealed through mine. I'm praying that you will be able to read between the lines of heartache and brokenness and visualize the hope, grace, and mercy of God. I want you to believe that He is working all things according to His plan for your good.

C—Circumstances:

The conditions that affect somebody's life that are beyond his or her control; the way an event happens or develops.

R—Reality:

Something that has real existence and must be dealt with in life; actual being or existence as opposed to imaginary.

A—Application:

The relevance or value that something has, especially when it is applied to a specific field or area. The process of putting it to use.

P— Purpose:

The reason for which something exists or for which it has been done or made. The goal or intended outcome of something.

He lifted me out of the ditch,
pulled me from deep mud.
Psalm 40:2

DYSFUNCTION BY DESIGN

CIRCUMSTANCE

I was born into the home of an alcoholic. My parents had six children. I was second to the youngest, if anyone was counting. I didn't get to choose which home I would be born into. If so, I would have chosen to be born into Carol's home. She was my friend from church. Her daddy was important. He wasn't the pastor, but he had a title and everyone respected him. She always had new clothes, they drove in a nice car, and they lived in a brick house. Why couldn't I be Carol?

Sometimes on Sundays, she would invite me over to her house for lunch and to hang out until we returned for the evening service. I was so excited! That meant I would have a really good lunch (one that included meat) and that I would get to see her room, which was always decorated beautifully. It also meant the other girls in church would think I must be okay. If she invited me over, I appeared to be normal. But I would never be like her.

No, I was just Judy. I don't know how my mother survived raising six children and living with an alcoholic. The children ranged in age between newborn to 9 yrs. My earliest memories are not the stuff of fairy tales. Children of alcoholics live extremely complicated lives. The devastation of normalcy required a continual front of secrecy. The desire to appear normal was overwhelming, and felt impossible to accomplish. In hopes of creating a picture of the true reality, allow me to describe a few childhood events.

At least once a month, we would enjoy what I like to call a "sing-a-long" with daddy. He would come in around 2:00am singing a loud version of some country song he had heard at the bar. Then he would systematically open our bedroom doors and insist that we get up and come into the living room. He wanted to hear his kids sing. Yes, we are a family of saints, sinners, and singers.

We would sing every song we knew. Some we had written, some momma had written, and then we would sing the songbook. "Melodies of Praise" was the old hymnal one of us had brought home from church. The singing usually lasted a good two hours. Then dad would become "happy" enough to sing bass for our closing song, "Joshua Fought the Battle of Jericho." Dad would begin marching around the living room in a circle and we would fall in line behind him. Finally, mom would convince him to allow us to get some sleep, because we had school tomorrow. Tomorrow was in a few hours.

Imagine the exhaustion of a first grader who had been up singing all night long. The classroom is an environment created for discovery and learning, but for us, it was an atmosphere of rest. We were finally in a safe place and we could relax just enough to fall asleep. Of course the teacher viewed our behavior as rude and disrespectful. How could I tell her what my life was really like? I didn't want my friends to know my daddy was different—that I was different.

Then there were the nights that were really exciting, the nights when dad had been "hitting the hard stuff." If momma felt like dad's behavior was becoming a little too hard to handle, she would sneak into the boy's room and get my oldest brother Michael to slip into the bathroom and climb out of the window. Then she would sneak one child at a time out of the window into his arms and eventually we would all be on our way.

We would walk about two-and-a-half miles to the "Tejas Motel." The manager there felt sorry for us and would allow my mom and us to stay in one of the rooms if there were any available. The "Tejas Motel" was not the Hilton. It was frequented for the use of profitable businesses which operated at night. There were two beds in the room. Mom would put three boys in one bed, three girls in the other and she would sleep on the filthy floor. When I think of those nights, it breaks my heart to realize that my precious mother had to sleep on the floor of a dirty motel just for the peace of mind that her children could rest.

We would return home the next day, going in the house just after we sent Michael in to see if daddy had gone to sleep yet. We knew things would be fine if he had just gone to sleep. Sometimes our things would be broken and the house would be a mess because it had made him angry when he discovered we had disappeared. We just tiptoed around and cleaned it up before any of the neighbors could see.

Now that I think of it, why did it matter if they could see? Obviously, they could hear the play-by-play the night before. Everyone wants people to believe that their family is normal right? We didn't choose to tell our neighbors everything. We simply explained away the circumstances and laughed it off. Laughter is a good cover. We simply developed the ability to play like everything's okay.

So many nights, the police would arrive on our front porch because a concerned neighbor had heard a "raucous" going on next door. Mom would insist everything was alright. Usually, that was enough to make the police go away. But one time, an officer actually asked if he could come in and take a look around. He opened our bedroom doors and asked us if we were okay. What were we going to say? "Yes, this is normal." Or, "No, please arrest our dad and make our mom cry some more." Really, what did he expect us to say? They would always leave without doing much. I'm not sure what I wanted. Did I want them to take me away? Did I want them to take daddy away?

Then there were the trips. Our Grandparents lived in Oklahoma. Several times a year we would be awakened with the announcement: "I'm leaving in twenty minutes, get your bags packed." We knew that meant another drunk-driving all night adventure. We must have been a sight driving around in the old junkers we had. Picture Dad, Mom, and Michael in the front seat and five of us piled up on each other in the back. Don't worry, that was way before the seat belt law went into effect. Janice or Jimmy were usually up on the back dash asleep and Kirley typically ended up in the floor board.

There was no air conditioning, so ordinarily we could hang our long legs out the window. Daddy really was a good driver. He was only stopped a few times by the highway patrol. I think they just wanted to see what was in the leg mobile. They never questioned if he was drinking. I guess they figured anyone with that many kids in the car would be driving crazy anyway.

Growing up in this type of environment was interesting to say the least. As I became a teenager, I developed a whole new set of coping skills. My first date was interesting. It was a Saturday night. Dad was well lit and insisted the young man come inside to meet him. After a session of Twenty Questions, as we were walking out the door,he announced, "She's not on the pill yet son!" (Just bury me here, I thought.)

Don't get me wrong. My daddy tried to be a good daddy. He always kept a job. He worked 3:00pm to midnight. This enabled him to leave work, pick up his alcohol on the way home, and sit up all night drinking. He would go to sleep around 7:00am and then get up by 2:00pm and start over. Of course there were some days he just couldn't make it in but he had plenty of sick days and vacation time. We never actually took a vacation. The trips to Oklahoma were all the "vacation" we experienced. They were definitely "experiences."

As you can see, Daddy had a strong work ethic. He made sure his children knew how to work. One Saturday a month we were up at the crack of dawn moving the board pile. Yes. We had a huge pile of wood out behind our house. Dad had built a stand to stack boards on, not logs, actual boards. Our job was to move each board one at a time to the other side of the yard and re-stack them in perfect order. It was hot work and we were exhausted by the time lunch was ready. Then, it was yard work for the boys and housework for the girls. I don't have a problem with children working around the house,it was the strict supervision and endless instruction that made the chores so difficult. We would wash the same load of dishes, by hand, (we never had a dishwasher)—-one dish at a time over and over until they were spotless. Bed-making and rug-sweeping also required strict training. (We also never had a vacuum).

If we weren't moving the "wood" pile, we were learning specific life skills needed to survive. Each of his girls was required to change all four tires on the car four times each. We were not going to be stranded with a flat tire and no one to change it. The boys were trained in the delicate art of knot tying. They were trained to tie specific knots in ropes while standing or lying in challenging positions. They could tie any sailor's knots behind their back.

Christmas was always interesting. We had a tradition of putting up the tree. Most of the time, we didn't get one until a few nights before Christmas. Dad would take the boys and go find a tree. Typically, it was taken from a lot at the end of our street but we didn't care, it was Christmas and we had a tree.

The fun started as we were instructed one by one to string the lights at certain intervals apart. Next, each of us were given a certain number of decorating balls and instructed to hang them in strategic locations to balance out the tree. This was always followed up by a designated few carefully placing one icicle at a time on each limb. When the tree was complete, Momma would hang the angel. Not a star, always an angel. Angels were holy, and trust me, angels were needed.

We would then sing every Christmas carol ever written followed by every song in the song book again and yes, close out the night with "Joshua Fought the Battle of Jericho."

Singing was something we truly enjoyed, it was therapeutic. All six of us took our turn singing in church programs and school choirs. We had such talent that even when we couldn't afford the costume or choir uniform someone would "sponsor" us. Usually it was the director, because they needed our voices and our ability to harmonize. All those late night singings taught us something of value.

The three younger children, Jimmy, Janice, and I, were able to participate in several musical performance groups. We lived for opportunities to sing and it became a perfect escape from the stress of home life. Except for those rare occasions when Dad would decide to attend a performance, which was usually a church service.

He would slip in the back and sit on the back row. You could hear him call out a few encouraging cheers between songs. Usually something like, "that's my baby" or "show 'em how it's done, son." Of course everyone turned to glare, but we found comfort in the knowledge that he would always leave before the altar call was over, so the audience was left to wonder whose dad that was making such a scene. Well, the ones who didn't already recognize who he was.

Sounds crazy, but there was a small part of me that was pleased he had come. That part of me that wanted my daddy to think I was special. I really wanted his approval,and I needed his attention. It's easy to get lost among six children in the house.

There are some experiences I truly appreciate about my childhood years with Dad. Though he was absent from my real world most of the time, on occasion he would check on each one of us before he went to bed to make sure we were warm enough or cool enough. I was very sickly and tended to run fever a lot.

Some of my most cherished memories would have to be of the nights I was feeling so weak and sick. The door would open; he would walk across the room, bypassing both of my other sisters, and place his huge hand on my forehead. I played like I was asleep but trust me, in my heart I was grinning from ear to ear. He really does care about me.

There are a few defining moments I can recall with clarity. The night before I graduated from high school, Dad had been out drinking again and came in around 2:30am. He came to my room and told me to come outside, he wanted to talk to me a minute. He said to be quiet, not to wake Momma.

I promptly dressed and slipped outside to the front yard. He had pulled his truck up into the yard, right in front of the porch and told me to get in. I climbed up in the truck and he began to cry. I could see a bottle of whiskey in his hand so I knew he had been "hittin' it hard" again. I was simply going to patronize him. This was a difficult time for him and he just needed to vent.

Big events were difficult for him to deal with. He felt like he had failed us and he didn't know how to tell us he was sorry. He knew he couldn't pay for us to attend college and he hadn't made arrangements for a graduation present. I was okay with that, really. I had learned to expect nothing; it was just better that way. I was crying though. I guess the events leading up to graduation day had worn me out. Life was not turning out like I would have dreamed, but dreams were not common in the world I lived in. I was tired and emotional but I wasn't expecting what happened next.

Without warning, the porch light came on and Momma stepped outside. She was furious with him. When she saw he had me in the truck and that I was crying, she lost it. I had never seen her act like this. She stormed over to his side of the truck, reached in the window and grabbed the bottle of whiskey from his hand. She walked back over to the porch and broke the bottle, then threw what was left across the yard.

She walked to my side of the truck, opened the door, and told me to go to bed. I quickly obliged and so did dad. He never said another word. He got out of the truck, went into the house, washed his face, and went to bed. He did make it to my graduation and yes, he was sober.

One of the final encounters I can remember from my years at home was the day I told Daddy I was going to get married. I remember it as though it was yesterday. He was seated in a brown recliner in front of the TV. I told him I needed to talk to him and he said, "Wait for the next commercial." I was so nervous, I was kind of thankful for a delay. I knew he wasn't going to agree with my decision.

When I told him I was going to marry "Bubba," his response was one of confusion. "Who are you talking about? That kid that plays the drums?" I replied, "Yes, Daddy you know, the boy who's played the drums for us the last four years." He used a few colorful words and insisted, "He's just a kid, Judy! He isn't even out of high school, is he?" What could I say? "No, but he graduates this year."

He sat quietly for a few moments then looked straight into my eyes. "Baby, are you pregnant?" This time I don't think he was joking. "No daddy, I promise I'm not." He sat back in his chair and mumbled a few curse words. Then he gave me his answer. "You can marry him if you want to but don't expect me to be there!"

I began to cry. "Daddy, don't do this to me." His next few words were familiar to me. When he couldn't handle the conversation anymore, this was his response. "I don't want to talk about it, not another word." I stood up to him for the first time ever. I said, "Daddy, I love you. I'm going to marry him if you're there or not, but I want you to be there." He simply shook his head "no" and I walked out of the house.

I'm sincere when I say my Daddy was a good man at heart. He came around. A few days before the wedding he called me over to his chair and asked me what I wanted him to wear to walk me down the aisle. I hugged his neck and told him he could wear anything he wanted. Then I looked in his eyes and I whispered, "Daddy, please don't be drinking at my wedding."

I should have covered the wedding rehearsal in my request. When he arrived that night he had been drinking and he was already ready for it to be over. I will never forget him pulling me to the side and asking me two things.

First of all, "What is that boys name anyway?" He had only heard us call him "Bubba." I said, "Oh yea, I'm sorry Daddy, his name is Robert." His next question was, "Does Robert always talk to his Momma like that?" My dad was very observant even when he was drinking. He wanted to know this boy was going to treat his daughter right. With respect. I admired his questions.

Yes. Daddy was sober for my wedding. Hungover and red faced, but sober. The last thing he said to me before we walked down the aisle was, "It's not too late, we can still leave." I kissed his cheek and said, "No daddy, this is what I really want."

February 4, 1967

I'm trying so hard to go to sleep but I just can't. It's already 1:30am and daddy's not home yet. He gets off work at midnight. You know that means he's at the bar. I can see his headlights when he gets home because they light up the whole room. The driveway's right outside the window.

Sshhh. There he is. I just heard him tell momma to get up - he wanted something to eat. That's a good sign. If he eats he'll sober up. (That's what mom says.) Well, now he's yelling at her again. It scares me because I'm afraid he might hurt her. She says he doesn't hit her but he always makes her cry. He makes me cry too.

He just woke the boys up. He was shouting orders at them to take the trash out. I guess they forgot again. Momma said it wasn't their fault but dad said they never do nothin' right but get in trouble. It won't hurt 'em to get their hands dirty. It sounds like Michael said something he shouldn't. Dad said he has to stay up. He's yelling at him for not respecting him. He's supposed to say, "Yes, sir." Now he has to say it over and over. It sounds like he's said it now at least a hundred times. Momma's asking daddy to let him go to bed now. Daddy told her to shut up but he did let Michael go to bed.

Momma says when I'm scared like this I should say the name of Jesus over and over till I fall asleep. Jesus, Jesus, Jesus… sometimes it works, sometimes it doesn't. I don't know how my sisters can sleep through this. I'm so tired but I can't go to sleep till he does. Why does he do this? Sometimes I think I hate him. Momma says not to hate him. She says we should hate the devil that makes him drink but we should always love our daddy.

OK. The T.V. is on now. Maybe he'll calm down. I think momma went back to bed. It's almost 4:00am now. I really am tired and I have to go to school in 3 hours. Jesus, Jesus, Jesus…

Alcoholism is considered a disease. It is also considered an addiction. Treatment programs such as Alcoholics Anonymous help people with alcohol dependence to stop drinking and improve their lives. Families of alcoholics need treatment just as much as alcoholics. Marriage and family counselors can help with the tensions created in the alcoholic's home. School counselors can provide information and support to adolescents who have family problems because of parental alcoholism. Hospitals and mental health center programs provide information and services for alcohol-related problems.

There are two organizations designed to treat the families of alcoholics. Al-Anon was created to treat the spouses of alcoholics and Alateen is designed to help children of alcoholics. Both organizations' philosophies are based on Alcoholic Anonymous' Twelve-Step Recovery Program. The main goal of these organizations is to help family members understand that they are not responsible for an alcoholic's drinking problems and that their recovery does not depend upon the alcoholic's recovery. Alcohol affects each member of the family. Its far-reaching effects result not only in physical problems for the alcoholics, but also may result in physical and psychological problems for other members of the family. Treatment is complicated and often is not completely successful. Even if the alcoholic himself ultimately reforms, the family members who were so greatly affected may not themselves ever recover from the problems inflicted upon them.

I believe that our own personal choices decide how our lives will turn out. I don't believe we can change the outcome of our circumstances by finding someone to blame. Though irrevocable damage is done, the world is full of damaged people who are actually surviving life. My personal opinion is most of the time, it is that very brokenness that pushes us into addictions. However, each of us ultimately decides how we will respond to the hand that is dealt to us.

Children of alcoholics are more likely to have problems in school. The stressful environment at home prevents them from focusing on their studies. Their school performance may also be affected by an inability to express themselves. Frequently, they will have difficulty in establishing relationships with others around them. These children struggle with behavioral problems such as lying, fighting, and stealing.

Living in extremely unstable home environments, they never know what to expect from an alcoholic parent. Because they are unable to predict their parent's actions, they don't have appropriate role models to follow. Their lives are spent trying to find new ways to please their alcoholic parent. They may become overachievers or withdraw into their own world. They may tiptoe around the house while the alcoholic parent sleeps, hoping not to awake the drunken person until enough time has passed for the alcoholic parent to "sober up." Children of alcoholics usually lack vision for their future. It is difficult to plan for college when you're not sure you will even make it through high school.

Statistics:

Children of alcoholics are four times more likely than other children to become alcoholics themselves.

Alcohol is a key factor in

- 86% of homicides

- 60% of rapes

- 48% of robberies

- 44% of burglaries

- 70% of domestic abuse

Children of alcoholics may be more likely to be the targets of physical abuse and to witness family violence. If healthy family rituals or traditions, such as vacations, mealtimes, or holidays, are highly valued and maintained and if there are consistent significant others in the life of the child or children there is a greater chance of emotional survival. Children need to be protected from many of the consequences of parental alcoholism. Most children of alcoholics have experienced some form of neglect. --See National Association for Children of Alcoholics

There have been several creative ideas developed to try to help in the overall challenges of alcohol addiction.

- There is a great need for community organizations and churches to become more involved in helping dysfunctional families cope. Intervention programs, child guidance, and coping skills classes, along with academic tutoring could develop a support system for the family unit. Life coaching classes and venting forums have proven effective.

- Safe Stay Locations would be of great benefit to a family looking for a nights stay. Waiting for a loved one to sober up is much easier in a quiet, protected place. Hotels could establish a safe haven room for low cost or no cost. Applications could be made in advance and management could offer the use of one vacant room. Churches or community centers could do the same.

- Some school systems are developing workshops and seminars teaching staff how to recognize and deal with children of alcoholics and addicts. Behavioral problems are so often misunderstood and then handled inappropriately. This only adds to the problem.

- Several authors have developed curriculum for the children of alcoholics. It would be beneficial to have a larger assortment of books written on a child's level that assists them in coping with their reality.

- Health care agents would be a helpful arm of support in the area of working with spouses and children of alcoholics. The amount of stress dealt with on a daily basis in the home takes a toll on the physical body. As physicians and nurses observe the physical effects, additional vitamins and care instructions could be offered. Suggestions for additional rest or exercise may make major lifestyle improvements.

- Police officers see it all. Additional consideration could be given to repeat domestic violence cases. Assistance in transport to a safe place while a loved one sobers up could prove helpful. Obviously, child protective services are not always necessary for occasional one nighters. However, thorough assessment of the situation may bring to light the severity or volatility of specific incidents.

- Tougher laws regarding drunk driving. Could we consider passing laws that would mandate higher penalties for adults driving drunk with children in the vehicle? If we already have those laws could we stiffen them?

- If we know that domestic violence occurs more often when alcohol or drugs are involved, could we expand the occasions we offer rehabilitation as a requirement for less jail time?

- Currently, rehab is quite expensive in many places. More outpatient programs with support would help to keep the costs down and encourage people to try to rehabilitate.

purpose

Sometimes, the greatest heartaches are the sharpest tools for creating the greatest masterpieces. I know that I am not the only little girl who grew up in less than perfect surroundings. I truly believe God knew everything about me before I was even born. He knew I was a twin sister before my parents or even the doctors knew. My brother was born seven minutes before I was. Everyone, including the doctor, was shocked to discover my feet. They had no idea my mother had carried twins to full term. Surprise!

The childhood I experienced prepared me for the work I am involved in today. I don't believe my work is a result of my childhood, I believe my childhood was preparation for my work. My purpose in life was being developed as I was struggling to find my identity. My heavenly Father used my earthly father to teach me truths that would affect my decisions for years to come.

I can now sit down beside a child who lives in the home of an alcoholic and tell them my story. I can laugh with them and cry with them as they share theirs. I have become a living example of hope to dysfunctional families. I'm living proof that God can take what feels like torment and use it to bring good things to pass for you.

Today, I have a beautiful life. I have an awesome, honorable husband who loves me, protects me, and provides for me. I have two beautiful daughters who make my life complete and live lives that honor me. I am surrounded by great friends and I am living my dream. When hurting children see me and hear my story, hope wakes up in their hearts and they find courage to keep going.

If you have never experienced this kind of home life, you cannot completely relate on the same level with people who have lived it. I will be effective at reaching out to children and families of alcoholics with empathy and a true understanding of what their lives are really like. What greater joy is there than to look into the eyes of a hurting child, see yourself there, and know you can offer hope? I was created for a purpose and developed with that purpose in mind.

I have it all planned out-plans to take care of you, not abandon you, plans to give you the future you hope for.
Jeremiah 29:11

PRICELESS POVERTY

CIRCUMSTANCE

"Poverty" is defined by Webster as, "the state or condition of having little or no money, goods, or means of support; condition of being poor; indigence." Poverty denotes serious lack of the means for proper existence. Okay. Well, maybe Mr. Webster took his notes from observing my home.

I am not choosing to whine because I grew up with nothing. I am trying to utilize the disgusting conditions of my formative years in proving that God works in every matter. I cannot separate my life now from the experiences of my life then. I make choices today based on the memory of those years. Allow me to formulate a picture of what I call alcohol- or drug-induced poverty.

We lived in two different houses from the time I was born till I moved out on my own as a young adult. I vaguely recall the first home I lived in. I know it was a small wood frame house that was located close to a creek. There were broken down cars parked around the perimeter and a huge dog house out back. I have a few pictures of myself and Jimmy, my twin, posing in the backyard and there appears to be some tires stacked up behind us.

I have to form my ideas based on stories that have been shared with me in regard to the first few years. I understand that our neighbors felt sorry for us and would occasionally buy us groceries. There was a friend who would watch us while another friend would take mom out to find dad. I do not have any real memories of that first house other than the excitement of moving day.

We had been evicted for non-payment of rent and dad had managed to find a guy who would owner finance an old fixer upper located a few blocks away. We were going to go and see the new house. I was only four, but I can truly remember the excitement of walking into that empty house and discovering the new place I would call home.

It was another wood frame home and had obviously been vandalized. There were two huge holes in the living room walls. The landlord said the prior tenants had knocked each other through the walls. Dad said he could build some shelves there and no one would know the difference. The room behind it was the garage and he had plans to close that in so it could be part of the renovations. The kitchen actually had a working stove in it. That was exciting to mom.

There was one small restroom that was located between two other small bedrooms and the back porch had broken off from the house. Dad said he could rebuild it. There were two doors on the front of the house. The screens were torn out and the steps there were broken also, but hey, it was to be our home and we would make it better than ever! The arrangement was that dad would fix it up for the down payment. We would move in immediately and begin the repairs.

Repairs were something that became a part of our lifestyle. For several years, dad would come home with some old wood he had acquired from friends or some old construction site. He and the boys would work late into the night while the girls would bring him beer and the boys iced tea. The leadership skills and determination of my dad would usually run out at about the same time as the beer.

It would be obvious the next morning that one of the walls was crooked or in need of rebuilding. Finally, after two-and-a-half years, the garage wall was completed with two cute little shelves for mom to put her clowns on. The boys could now sleep in the garage room instead of on the living room floor. It was only about ten-by-eight feet, and it was extremely cold in the winter and very hot in the summer. But it was the boy's room and they were proud of it! Dad and Mom shared the middle room and 3 of us girls shared the back room.

We didn't have an air conditioner so we utilized box fans. Once in a while, when we were experiencing a really hot summer, dad would get just drunk enough to spend the rent money to get an old water cooler from the pawn shop. Those were wonderful days. I loved the smell of the cool air as it would fill the living

room. Mom would hang an old quilt over the opening to the kitchen and we would close off all the other rooms. It was like heaven in the middle of hell.

Of course, in a few days it would mysteriously disappear and we would be back to the box fans. To this day, I find it completely impossible to fall asleep without a fan blowing across my face.

The restroom renovations were the most trying for our family. Every other weekend dad would have to fix the drainage problem with the plumbing. This meant he would remove the toilet and the bathtub from the restroom while he and the boys used shovels to try and discover what was blocking the pipes.

The problem was that he would get too drunk to finish the project and we would have to wait a week for him to finish the job. This was to become a continual process. We had no alternative. If we needed to use the restroom facilities, we were to use the hole left in the floor that led into the toilet drainage pipe. As you can imagine, this was much easier for the 3 boys than it was for us girls.

We could utilize the coffee can, but that meant we would have to pick it up to empty it and for a girl, that was the ultimate grossness. It's not easy having a nervous stomach and developing the skills required to squat and aim. Sounds difficult, and it was. But you do what you have to do.

The absence of a tub was handled well. Necessity is the mother of invention, right? Well, Dad would line us up out in the front yard with a bar of soap and we would wash while he sprayed us down with the water hose. That was fun for the young ones, but as we grew older it became embarrassing. It is difficult to wash your hair with a bar of soap and a water hose considering there is only one temperature, cold.

Luckily, dad would get the tub back in and working quicker than the toilet. Mom needed the tub because that was our washing machine. She would fill the tub with soapy water, place our clothes inside and, utilizing the toilet plunger she would beat the dirt out of them until they were good and clean. Then she would repeat until they were rinsed. For a while it was fun helping her "wring them out" but with six kids, that's a lot of wringin'.

We didn't have a dryer so they would hang outside on the clothesline. When we became teenagers, things became real complicated. We had to wash them at night and lay them across the oven door to dry in the heat, that is, if the gas was actually turned on that week. Because we wore the same clothes so often, we didn't have time to hang them on the line.

Utilities were dad's specialty. The water would be cut off almost every other month. He had a tool that could be used to cut it back on. We would watch for the water man to get back in his truck and drive off and then daddy would walk out to the street remove the cement lid, reach down into the hole and magically, the water would work again for a few days.

One summer, mom had decided it was too much. She packed up everything she could in trash bags and had her sister drive down from Oklahoma to pick us up. She decided to move us in with her mother and try to get a job and make it on our own. I was only in the second grade but I remember that year so well.

She got a job at the "Dairy Cup," a small burger place in Seminole, OK. Every once in a while, rather than dispose of the items left at the end of the night shift, they would allow Momma to bring them home. We were so excited to see what she had. Cold burgers, hot dogs, or left over ice cream in a used bucket. We loved it!

Mom found a small three room house located by a pond at the end of a very small street. She had to have been looking really hard to locate this place. She felt like it was important that we move out of Grandma's house, so we walked up the hill carrying everything we owned and moved into this run down, sad little place. I cannot name the emotion I am feeling even now as I am describing it.

There was a train track located very close and I could hear the train whistle and horn blow all hours of the night. To this day, I choose not to live close enough to a train that I can hear it in my home. When I hear that sound, my heart sinks and I feel an overwhelming sadness. Sound tied to memory is a powerful thing.

It was so cold that winter, the pond nearby would freeze up and you could hear the sound of trees cracking and breaking just outside the window. I was so fearful a tree would crash through the house while we were sleeping; I spent many nights awake, watching and waiting.

The bus didn't run on our street so we walked home from school. Yes, it really was uphill in the snow. I was a sickly child so you can imagine how often that winter I was running a fever and we could not afford medicine. We would get inside the house and realize the pipes that brought water to our home had frozen. We could not go anywhere until mom came home from work. I recall being so thirsty that I would actually go to the window and lick the condensation off the glass. It was cold and at least it wet my cracked lips and quenched my thirst for a while. In Oklahoma, single mothers and poor people received what was called "commodities" from the government. It was a box full of free groceries. There was a lot of peanut butter. I distinctly remember how sick I was of eating it. We were taught to be thankful, but I couldn't take another spoon of it.

During that year, I began to withdraw. I was embarrassed to be known as the poor girl at school. Children are cruel if they are not taught to be kind. I lied to my mom for the first time in second grade. All the girls in gym class had hula hoops. I didn't have one so I couldn't play, I just watched them play. I was too shy to ask if I could play with them. So, I thought about it all the way home and that night I told Momma the teacher said I had to have a hula hoop for gym class.

Momma walked in the cold dark night to grandma's house to borrow $1.79 to walk further down the street to the dime store to buy me the hula hoop. I don't think I ever told her about that lie, but I remember it to this day every time I see a hula hoop.

That spring, Michael, the oldest child, left home for the first time at the age of 14. He was missing and Momma was so scared. He was only a teenager and she cried for what seemed to be weeks. She called Daddy and found out that he had made it home to live with Dad. A boy needs his Dad and she resolved to let him stay.

A few months later, Dad called and talked Mom into coming back home. He promised to sober up and make things better. In desperation, she accepted the invitation and we moved back to Texas. He had actually gotten a much better job and was doing better. His drinking continued, but at least he was making enough money to help make the house payment, most of the time.

The house we moved back into was the same. The pipes continued to clog and the ongoing job of toilet in–toilet out haunted us for years. Our door handles were unique. When one broke, we simply tied an exquisite knot in a sock, stuck it through the hole and used it for a door handle. We learned to boil water for baths and to drain the tub with a water hose. It's amazing what you can do when you have to.

Our church was our greatest means of support in those days. Mom would not ask for help but they could see the need. There were so many Christmases when Santa came and dropped off a black trash bag full of toys bought by the church families. Groceries were often quietly placed in brown paper sacks on our porch or someone would sneak them into the church and put our name on them.

I recall once, I was only about eight years old and the Missionettes, the little girls Bible class from our church had planned a trip to Six Flags. I had gathered coke bottles and exchanged them for nickels to save enough money for my trip. It took weeks and weeks of saving but I had sacrificed to make it happen because I had heard of Six Flags but never imagined I would ever get to go.

I could barely sleep the night before in anticipation of what it would really be like. As soon as I realized the sun was up, I jumped up and threw on the clothes I had carefully laid out the night before. When I went into the kitchen, I moved a chair over by the fridge to climb up and collect the jar of money I had been saving. It was empty!

Dad had taken the money during the night to make his second run to the beer store. I was so crushed at that moment. I thought he loved me. Why, why would he do this to me? I struggled in my 8 year old mind to try and make sense of his actions. I was enraged and fractured. My heart was overwhelmed with mixed feelings of hate and guilt for hating. My eyes were burning with tears as I was startled by the honk of a horn out front. They had come to pick me up for the trip and now I couldn't go. I sat crying as Momma walked out to the street to let them know I would not be able to go. She was out there for what seemed an eternity.

When she came back in, she smiled and grabbed my shoes. She said "Hurry, get these on...you get to go!" The leaders had pooled their money to pay my way. My life was affected by two different forces that day. Good and Evil. Good triumphed, I hardly remembered the unspeakable anger I had felt just moments before. Six Flags was wonderful, plus I was given ten dollars to buy souvenirs. It was life changing.

Whatever your circumstances, you find ways to make things work. With six children, I'm sure my mom felt she had no choice. Eventually, she got a job working at the same factory where dad worked. She took the morning shift and he worked the evening. They never saw each other but that was okay. The kids were old enough to get themselves dressed for school and she could be home in the afternoons a few hours after we returned.

We didn't mind. We believed it would mean more money in the household and more of the things we needed. It didn't slow down dad's drinking, but it did provide for a few more pairs of jeans and panties.

We didn't have meat for dinner except for Sundays. On occasion, we did get to have hamburgers on payday and sometimes we could even get a large bottle of Pepsi. We didn't get to buy our lunches at school and Momma didn't sign us up for the free meal tickets. I wasn't sure why she didn't. However, we did take sack lunches. We had to use the same sack until it tore up but at least we had something to eat.

Mom would make these homemade yeast rolls. They were awesome—at first. But after taking yeast rolls and peanut butter to school every day for months, I simply chose not to eat. My brother Jimmy came up with a great plan. He began trading the peanut butter rolls for other people's lunch money. The rolls really were good and he could then buy pizza!

Middle school was always very difficult for us. Adolescence is deadly. Peer pressure was nothing compared to humiliation and just plain brutal bullies. Boys and girls both develop the skill of saying and doing cruel things for the sake of fitting in. Those located at the bottom of the socio-economic ladder were the ones who most often suffered the inhumane degradation of teenage insults and actions. We never invited friends to our home to visit. Our fear was they would laugh at our living conditions or dad would come in drunk and embarrass us.

We didn't get school clothes at the beginning of each year like a lot of kids. Occasionally, we would get excited at the chance to go to Kmart and purchase socks and panties. We were just glad some friends at the church would clean out their closets to make room for their new clothes and give us their old clothes . We shared everything from panties to jeans. This worked well until the kids in junior high choir recognized that my brother Jimmy was wearing the jeans I had worn the day before. That was certainly humiliating. For both of us.

It's great to give and to receive hand-me-downs. I don't know how we would have lived without them. However, might I encourage the givers to teach their children not to point out that Judy is wearing my Mom's old dress during Bible class? Please don't read this as ungrateful. My favorite hand-me-downs were from my Pastor's wife's closet. My sisters and I would always argue over who got to look in the bag first! She gave us the most beautiful things.

Looking back now, I can see so many areas where my mother sacrificed for us. She never purchased anything new for herself. Dad would not remember her birthday or their anniversary until a few days later, and then he would call her from work and tell her, "I left a ten on the table, go get a new bra or something". At Christmas, we would each get a dollar to go and buy her something. Each of us would purchase a small clown or a picture of one because we knew how much she loved clowns. She had collected them for years. They have sad faces and happy faces. They teach us that life can be happy or sad; it's all in what you make it. True to life.

Mom worked several weeks of overtime one year. Imagine taking care of six children, cooking, cleaning, and laundry along with working a full-time job and trying to balance living with an alcoholic. But even in her exhaustion, love motivated her to work overtime. She wanted to buy an old used piano from a lady she met at work. She knew I had such a love for the piano. I would draw pictures of the black and white keys on notebook paper and then tape the papers to the dresser to allow my fingers to pretend that I was playing.

I would disappear at church and she would find me playing the piano. So, she made it happen. My heart burst with excitement the day that piano was carried in. There were so many arguments caused by my desire to play and my families desire to watch TV. Oh yea, TV. Well, we didn't always have one. Only on the weekends it wasn't sitting in the pawn shop. Dad would frequently pawn the TV for drinking money. It was usually reclaimed in time for the football game to air. You can survive without a TV or a piano, but it's amazing how thankful you are to have them when it's not something you are accustomed to.

As an adult, I have discovered some disappointing truths. During those years of barely making it, my dad was actually making very good money. He was a Quality Inspector for a large manufacturing company. We were not poor because he didn't have a job or because he didn't get paid well, we were poor because he was an alcoholic and his need for alcohol was stronger than his need to provide for us. We didn't apply for government assistance or free lunches because even with six children, Dad and Momma made too much money to qualify. Yet, we suffered with such inadequate, degrading living conditions because he squandered away everything for the sake of another drink.

Eventually, his company called him in and offered an ultimatum, "Give up the alcohol or give up the job." Sadly, his children were already grown and out of his home before he made the decision. He went in for medical help, laid down the alcohol, and in the process he gained a disability from his job. Now, his home is the finest on the street. His refrigerator is full. His forty-two inch TV belongs to him and works with a remote. There are two cars in his driveway, fully paid for, and he has plenty of Pepsi. His home, however, is empty and quiet.

March 17, 1974

Oh, God I don't want to go to school today. I don't think I can face another day. I hate it. I hate those kids. I wish just once Renay would be absent. Just once, I wish she would find someone else to make fun of. I don't understand why they all like her so much. She is evil personified and she has a huge nose!

Mrs. Hearn my favorite English teacher is insisting we turn in those stupid journals. If I write what I really feel, she would die of shock. It's amazing how little she really knows about me. She thinks I'm like the others. I'm sure she imagines I live in a two story house like the Brady Bunch because there are six kids.... here's a story of a lovely lady...well, never mind. She can tell by the way I dress I don't live like Marsha.

Well, here I sit. 2nd period study hall. I'm looking around and wondering what everyone else did last night. Did they all have milk and cookies before they went to bed? Did they get to listen to their dad in the next room training the family dog with chains on the dining table? That would be fun...duh?

What I would give to live somewhere else...anywhere. Dad brought home a de-skunked skunk for a family pet. That works. The perfect dysfunctional animal for the perfect dysfunctional family. How drunk do you have to be to spend your drinking money on a skunk? Drunk as a skunk...I guess!

It's funny how I enjoy just writing out what I'm thinking. It's not like anyone will ever read it but it kind of feels like therapy... I can say anything I want and no one knows. I hate Renay. I hate Renay. I hate Renay. She told me a while ago that my hair would look better if I would part it on the side. Like I care what she thinks.

It does feel better to say it.... Someday, maybe I'll say it out loud. Your hair looks stupid. I don't care if you made the drill team. I don't care if you get to go to drill camp. I do like Carla though; she's nice when Renay is not around.

Often children who grow up in a life of poverty are affected by family stresses beyond their control. It is sad that a child would find themselves worrying about where the money for their school supplies is coming from or if they will have groceries next week. When it becomes obvious to others, the humiliation can be devastating.

Children are highly influenced by the shame that comes with living in poverty. Differences in socio-economic status are observed at an early age, which creates division from same-age peers. The ultimate humiliation suffered when friends discover how poor you are can be devastating to social development.

Most children desire to fit in with others but in some circumstances, they involuntarily stand out. In our society, there has always been a huge media blitz encouraging expensive brand-name clothing. Children are influenced by the culture they live in. They notice what others their age are wearing and desire to imitate that. The inability to purchase the latest style or fad causes them to stand out and be classified as poor. What a tag to wear around your neck.

Educational and social development are directly affected by the lack of confidence a child suffers when they are influenced by poverty. Poor self-esteem influences behavior and effects a child's confidence in their ability to succeed. Their class work suffers and they fail to earn opportunities for advancement in college or employment. Thus, the poverty cycle begins again.

What can we do?

- Change the atmosphere as early as possible. Environmental and developmental psychologists have studied how a child is affected by poverty. Environmental issues have a greater impact at a younger age.

- Studies have shown that the high levels of stress children in poverty experience affects brain structure and function.

- There is a great need for the positive friendships and supportive communities. The simple assurance of unconditional acceptance makes a huge difference in the way a child processes the devastation of poverty.

- Churches can be a very effective tool in coming alongside families in need of assistance. Not just a hand out but actually a hand up. Many houses of worship have set up food pantries and offer financial assistance with utilities and rent.

- Neighborhood partnerships go beyond the basics of Goodwill and The Salvation Army to establish community sharing and free thrift shops.

- Many communities offer backpack giveaways filled with school supplies and much-needed health screening and immunization coupons.

- We are paying a price for the inefficient way we connect with each other to deal with this issue. Once again, it's amazing that the answer for the need of the people is best met by the people. We must stop looking to our government to fix the poor.

- We must become proactive instead of reactive in serving our communities. It's important to develop ways of meeting the needs of children in poverty with dignity and create an atmosphere free of humiliation. Together, we can end the continuing cycle, one child at a time.

I am stunned today as I consider the differences in my life now, and the challenges I faced as a child of poverty. As a child, I could not even have dreamed of the amount of provision and material gifts I own today. My home is huge and beautiful. My clothes are paid for and my closet is full.

There is no way you could have convinced me that poverty or blessing was a part of God's plan. I loved Him enough to look to Him, but not enough to expect what I have now received. I hold back the tears as I allow myself to consider it all. I'm ashamed of my lack of thankfulness. I must walk away from my computer long enough to thank God for His hand in my life.

When I ask God to reveal His purpose of poverty in my life, I begin to understand why Jesus had to come to earth and live as a man. He was moved by the feelings of our infirmities. Because of my experiences of poverty, I truly hurt inside when I see a child who is being made fun of because their clothes don't fit or are not the right style.

My heart is broken when I realize there are children in my sphere of influence who do not know if they will have groceries this week. There are children whose prayer request every week is, "Help my Mommy and Daddy find a place for us to live". These are not just trite, little cute prayer requests to me. They are little lives crying out for help from a God who is bigger than their circumstances.

I do not have the finances to meet all their needs but I have a history of trusting a God who owns it all. I can assure these little children that God understands what they need and He will make a way for them. If I hear of a child who cannot afford to participate in a specific function, I am moved with compassion–not pity. I know the emotion they are feeling and I will not look the other way. God has taught me that His eye is on the sparrow. Just let me get closer to the sparrows.

The kingdom of heaven is like a little child. They need to know there is someone bigger than Mommy and Daddy who can and will meet their needs. It is my job to ensure they have heard that message. It is also my desperate desire to work with a team of people who will be as sensitive to the needs as if it were our own children. And, sometimes…it is.

All the stages of my life were spread out before you...
Psalm 139

ESTEEM EXTREME

CIRCUMSTANCE

There was a new wave of teaching developed back in the '70s & '80s that established the standard of developing healthy self-esteem in the lives of our children. The schools began to develop new rules for reward and punishment and our entire society changed the way they viewed parenting skills.

It was as though the most important thing to teach our children was that they were priceless and the entire world evolved around them. Okay, that may be a slight overstatement. However, it was a strong message that was soon adopted by every aspect of society. "Everyone on the team gets a trophy."

"Even if you don't pass the test you can have a sticker and try again."

This train of thought was supposed to bring about a new generation of highly-developed, over-achieving adults. What we have now instead are self-centered, manipulative, greedy, controlling illiterates. Okay, that may be a little overstated, but it is obvious that overcompensating in the area of self–esteem building does not bring about a successful culture.

At the opposite end of the spectrum, children of alcoholics struggle with self-esteem more than any other segment of society. Statistics have proven that children who grow up in an environment controlled by addiction almost always see themselves as failures.

As a young girl, I had a tendency to simply get lost in the crowd. With six children in a small home, it's really easy to do. I preferred to live in an imaginative place hidden in the room I shared with my sisters. While the others were watching cartoons, I would slip away and play like I was a singing star or a pretty actor in a commercial.

I would take sheets of used notebook paper and turn them over, tape them together, and draw a realistic piano keyboard. Then, I would tape it to the dresser, position myself at just the right angle in front of the mirror, and proceed to sing all of the sad songs I knew.

Sad songs were easier because I knew all the words and could sing them with feeling. I tried everything I knew to make myself look pretty in the mirror. I would take whatever red substance I could find, a marker, crayon, even left over kool-aid to make my cheeks pink and my lips red. I never really felt pretty but I did feel like I was someone else for a little while.

As a pre-teen, I discovered quickly what gets attention. Pretty hair, pretty nails, cool clothes and jewelry, these were the things that made you beautiful. All of the things I knew I would never have. I simply grew accustomed to borrowing a little make-up from a friend at school.

It was at the age of twelve that I discovered one other thing that would make me feel pretty. Boys. Yes, I will never forget the first kiss I received from Jamie, one of the neighborhood boys . I had physically developed a little quicker than some of the other girls, which made me the prize for first-kiss practice. That sweet relationship lasted all of about four hours. I wasn't thrilled and he was embarrassed, but at least we could say we had kissed.

Our neighborhood was full of kids discovering exciting firsts to try . We began to play the usual games of "spin the bottle" and "seven minutes in heaven." I wasn't the one everyone wanted to pick but at least I wasn't left out of the games. The older I was, the more brave I became.

I had such a desire to be included in a group any group would have been fine. I just wanted to know I was valued. I developed a sweet friendship with some girls who lived across the street. They accepted me for who I was. I truly believed they cared for me. I found approval in their eyes and friendship in their hearts.

We were all looking for something. We each had our own personal struggles to deal with and I could write an entire other book covering all of our issues. We enjoyed sharing girls' night sleepovers. But always at their home, I was far too smart to take a chance of having someone stay over at my house. Who knew when dad would come in drinking? And aside from that risk, I had too many brothers.

One night, we all decided that we wanted to get up early the next morning and head for the mall. "Big Town Mall" seemed like a huge place back then and the excitement of a challenge added to the "big" experience. We would split up into teams and see which team could steal the most without getting caught. I was all in. I truly enjoyed a good challenge and I knew with my above-average IQ, I could win this one hands down.

I was paired up with Sherry. Just my luck, the only girl in the entire group who would not sin! She was truly committed to her beliefs and there was no room for compromise. I wasn't too concerned; I liked her best and was fine having her as my partner. There was something that felt safe about shoplifting with a Christian. I was a Christian too, but at the time it was simply more important to be accepted than forgiven.

We were doing very well at our new-found challenge. Well, I was doing well. Sherry was extremely nervous and continually shared her worries with me. I did my best to calm her fears until the inevitable occurred.

We had cleared several major stores and were heading into the small jewelry boutique when a voice behind me spoke quietly. "How much did you pay for those bracelets you picked up at Montgomery Ward?"

I turned around to see a middle-aged man in a green leisure suit leering at me with a determined eye. I said quickly, "What bracelets?" That was it; Sherry started crying right then and there. His response, "The ones you just picked up." Taking Sherry's arm and pushing her out of the store, I spoke clearly this time, "I don't know what you're talking about."

Sherry was close to hyperventilation at this point as he walked close enough to take my other arm and show me his badge. I realized by this point it would be futile to make a scene, so I agreed to go back to the store's security office with him.

There we were, two young, adventurous girls sitting in the presence of the store manager and security officers. They asked Sherry to pour the contents of her purse onto a small table in the corner of the room. I will never forget what I saw. It was amazing to me., The entire stack of her most-prized possessions included a key ring, some flavored lip gloss, a cute little mirror compact, and yes, a bright red New Testament.

The manager and security officers smiled at each other as they realized that she was obviously innocent and so they opened the door and told her she could leave. She slipped out quickly and did not look back.

I wish I could say that I remained calm, but the realization that I was really in trouble for the first time in my life hit my racing heart. I knew what would happen when I emptied my purse, absent of any bibles. I had over $200.00 worth of merchandise in that bag but only one item had a price tag left on it——$5.89.

They were not able to charge me with more than the theft of $5.89 in value, but they decided to teach me a lesson and called the local police to come and take me down to the station. Okay. Now I had to do some quick thinking. I knew my dad was out of town and we did not have a working phone at our house. So when they asked if I wanted to call my parents, I simply stayed strong and silent while shaking my head, as if to personify a "no fear" mentality.

What did I say about my IQ? I did come to my senses and began trying to talk my way out of it. I got no deal with the security guard however, I did overhear him tell the policeman, "Go easy on her." Upon arriving at the police station, I had begun to cry. I'm sure it was becoming obvious to the officers that this was actually my first time to do anything this stupid.

I sat there and cried for over 2 hours. They didn't put me in a cell or restrict my ability to move around the office. They actually sat me at a table over in the corner and watched me cry. They were trying to get in touch with my family. I shared with them that my dad gets drunk a lot and goes out of town. I told them my mom was a Christian and she was going to kill me.

The neighbor girls had returned home, and in fear, told their parents what had happened. Their parents let my mom use the phone and she reached the officers in charge. They assured her that I had learned my lesson and that nothing would be put in my record.

I had reached the point of desperation. I wanted too much to be the one everyone wanted to be around. That day, I decided it wasn't worth the heartache it had caused my mother. She truly believed I was the one child who would never have made the choice I made that day. She could never tell my dad. He expected this of the boys but it would push him over the edge to know that I had done it. There's no telling what he would do when he was drinking. She couldn't take the chance.

I promised her with heartfelt honesty that I would never, ever do anything like that again. I meant it. I would never, ever again hurt her heart by making the wrong choices. Or at least that was my plan.

On the weekends, if we gathered enough coke bottles to sell at the corner grocery, we could go skating. The skating rink was a great place to go. Mom thought it was safe and I had finally discovered something I was good at—roller skating. She would take us girls and drop us off for the evening, then return to pick us up around 11:00 p.m. so we would be home in bed before Dad arrived home.

I was, along with my sisters and our friends, always on the lookout for a good-looking boy who might ask me to skate the "couple's skate" with him. My sisters always had someone to skate with, even before they called for that particular activity. I would wait until all the boys had been picked and then hopefully, one of the desperate ones would ask me to skate.

My sister Janice was beautiful. She was always the pick of the pack. My older sister, Kathy, knew so many of the boys she had no trouble finding a partner. I was the one lined up with the other wallflowers wishing someone would notice me until one evening, someone did. I later discovered that my sister felt so sorry for me she had approached him and offered to pay him if he would ask me to skate.

I was amazed at how well he could skate, and he was intrigued that someone would care enough for me to actually pay someone to give me attention. We became friends instantly and by the end of the evening we were fully involved in the corner of the rink. They called it "making out" back then; I call it one of the biggest mistakes I ever made. I'll call this mistake, Steven.

Low self esteem can have devastating effects on a child. The way we see ourselves influences our choices. Our choices shape our lives. The lives of the people living in my home were certainly devastated by life choices based on how we saw who we were.

I have asked my living brother and sisters to send me an email sharing with me how they perceived life growing up in a home of alcoholism and poverty. I wanted to hear how they would express the effect it had on their self esteem. I wanted them to describe their feelings and then see if their views matched mine. I find it interesting how well our opinions coincide.

Michael

Looking back, I can see very clearly how each of the children growing up in our family dealt with their own issues of low self esteem. Michael became a "hippie." He was the oldest of the bunch and he carried a load that was much too big for his shoulders. He had to serve as "dad" in a lot of ways. Too many times he had to help Momma shield the rest of us from the effects of Dad's drinking.

In the late '60s and early '70s it was cool to let your hair grow long, wear cut offs and experiment with drugs. This lifestyle choice eventually led him to leave home at an early age and get involved in the culture of sex, drugs, and freedom. It also landed him in prison for drug possession.

While experimenting with drugs was widely accepted during the years of "Flower Power," Michael's use of drugs led him into trouble. He had the kindest nature of all of the boys. He would do anything for you and his good heart motivated him to give away almost everything. But he became a totally different person when he was using illegal substances.

One summer, he was living at home for a few months. It was a hot afternoon in Texas, one of those days where you could hear the locusts chanting in the trees and smell the heat of the sun on the sidewalk. Mom was clearly upset about something so I sat down beside her to ask what was wrong. She had been praying with desperation and it was obvious things were critical. She explained to me that Michael was on something and he had taken the car. Her worry was that he would hurt himself because he was too messed up to drive. My ten-year-old mind was trying to reason why he would hurt her heart like this when suddenly my thought process was interrupted by a screeching sound outside.

Mom and I ran outside and discovered that Michael had returned. She began to call out to him, "Please park the car." He became irrational. He hit the gas and directed the car at Mom. I could not believe what I was seeing. I panicked and ran in front of her. The only thing that saved our lives was the small tree that blocked his view. He crashed right into it and I heard the engine roar as he tried to knock over the tree with the force of the car.

He jumped out of the car and began running down the street just as the police came around the corner. That day I discovered once again that drugs can transform a sweet and gentle man into a stranger I did not recognize. Later, years of involvement with illegal drugs placed him in a Santa Fe, New Mexico prison during one of the worst prison riots in history.

The prisoners had taken control of the prison, broken into the infirmary, and had begun torturing the guards and trustees. The news reports indicated that, "Blood was running in the halls and stalls." The aftermath photos were graphic and most could not be shown on the television newscast. Dad and Mom spent several days checking a list that was posted on the gate. It was a list of the dead they were able to identify.

Mike had the good sense to crawl up into an air conditioning vent and wait it all out. For more than three days he saw things through the vent that would affect his heart and mind for the rest of his life. When he was released from prison, he came home for a while and tried to make a real relationship work with the love of his life. Marie loved his tender heart but could not tolerate his alcohol and drug habit.

When his marriage was over, he took to the road again and found his place of acceptance on the street with the homeless. He tells me he prefers to live on the street. People don't judge you and you can make it with a little help from your friends. He finally found the acceptance he was looking for.

On several occasions, he has visited with us for dinners and holidays. At one of our last family get-togethers Mike got in the food line at the very end. I summoned him to the front of the line with the adults. His reply, "Oh, I'm just a tramp, I can wait my turn." It was such a clear statement of how he continues to view himself.

In his own words: (Mike's E-mail)

"The bad things in my childhood were the fact that we could never feel safe in our home. Due to the fact that we did not know what each day would bring. We had good and bad. But a lot of them that made us confused, because of the future we saw with father's drinking. It was fun but others scary. Since we were all young it seemed like there would never be an end to this. I was the oldest male in the bunch, and always worried about the young ones and Mom. And in return they worried about me. I tried to be the big brother but my father really did not give me time to be. The realty is a very deep emotion for me. And I really will talk to you Judy if you can call me. I am having Janice type this so you can have a little information for your idea. But if you need more please call me and let's talk in private… Love you sis."

Kathy

Kathy was the oldest girl, born three years after Michael. She was beautiful but struggled with accepting her own appearance. She would cry for hours in front of the mirror and Momma would try to convince her that her hair was pretty. It seemed that every day before school she would become upset and leave for class with swollen eyes. I thought she was pretty and cool. I wanted to wear her clothes and be a teen-ager just like her. But, I didn't want to make Momma cry like she did.

When you don't feel pretty, it's easy to accept less than you deserve from relationships. I believe all of the girls in our family spent most of our lives longing for a strong man who would protect and care for us. The absence of security and the lack of self esteem caused us to look for love in all the wrong places and we almost always came up losing.

Today, Kathy is happily married and has a wonderful relationship with her husband. She has raised four children. We talked recently regarding one of her sons who struggles with alcoholism. The effects of poor self esteem are always passed down from generation to generation. The best thing we can do for our children is to offer them unconditional love and pray for them continually. Just like Momma.

In her own words: (Kathy's E-mail)

"I guess if I were to try to explain the repercussions that were brought to my growing up period from being raised in a family with alcoholism; I would begin from the beginning. At times, I was angry, so angry that I would retreat into my own space. I wrote poetry about princesses and white knights and a place that was sunshine and roses. Other times I was so confused. It was scary to think that on one hand, God would get me if I did anything wrong, or Dad would if I wasn't perfect. Add to that Mom was a saint.

I always felt that I was never going to be good enough for anyone because I could not please God and please Dad and Mom at the same time. Let me see, how did this yoyo life affect me? I would have to say that it made me quite insecure. I wanted to be loved for myself. But I really did not feel like I pleased anyone. I was one of the kinds of students who had to work for my grades. I loved to prove to myself that I could get good grades. Then maybe Dad would love me and not yell. He really was the kind of guy who didn't pat you on the back to show his love. He was the kind who told you to stand up. Stand straight and tuck your feelings away. He was not one to show emotions in the normal kinds of things.

He was two guys to me. It is how I dealt. On the weekends, he was a stranger who talked to the dog at the kitchen table. He woke us up to talk to us at two or three in the morning. He was supervisor over a bunch of women and would talk to me about the ups and downs of working with women. (Mostly the downs.)

My father was the dad who wasn't drinking at the time and would let me stay home from church on Sunday night and watch Bonanza with him or would watch wrestling with me on Mondays. I loved to think of him as "Fritz von DeLo," he was always a strong bear of a man to me. He was tall, beefy, and had a great voice.

I certainly cannot blame my later mistakes on my dad. But my perceptions as a daughter were a little confused. As I got out of high school, I felt the need for some validation that someone could love me. When I was low I didn't drink, I looked for love, as they say.

I wanted someone to use as an escape route. Before I confuse you, let me digress. I met a guy in the 9th grade when we were separated from Dad. We moved to Oklahoma and I met a preacher, who went to Oklahoma University. I was crazy about him. He asked me to marry him when I graduated. I did. It was a fairytale come true until I found out that he had a roommate and only wanted to marry to cover up his love for another man. I found out a little too late. I was attacked and battered physically and emotionally. My dad and brothers came to my rescue.

Over the next six years I married two more times to men who were strong, in my warped sense of emotions. I grew to be afraid of my own shadow. I could not make my own mind up and finally grew enough in God and myself to walk away from an ever-increasing chain of bad decisions. How does one explain depression, self-loathing, and feeling dirty, while trying to walk in the presence of a God who was going to strike me dead for all my transgressions?

I finally decided that I needed to stand on my own. I had a job and two sons under the age of four. I walked away and in my own way grew up a bit. I still fight depressions and insecurities but I know that God is the reason I am still here today.

I finally met my match in a wonderful man who tolerates my faults and loves me unquestionably. We now have two more children and have raised them as one unit. I see myself in others, and pray daily God would help them out of the decisions that may cause them pain.

My father and I talked out our differences long ago and I have, and will always love him. We have lost other members of our family due to alcohol- and drug-related illnesses and bad decisions. But I find that through God's grace and our own experiences, it is possible to survive.

So dear sister, take this abridged version of my life story and I hope it blesses someone.

With all my love,

Kathleen"

Kirley

Kirley, born three years after Kathy, became the clown. He was the funny one. He compensated for his lack of self esteem by showing out and misbehaving. It didn't concern him if the teachers were upset, as long as the other kids thought he was funny. He would always break up the stress at home with some witty response or by singing a tune in a comical high-pitched voice.

After failing in school, Kirley dropped out and began spending too much time with the wrong crowd. His relationship with Dad suffered as the effects of alcoholism began to take its toll on both of them. A lot of Dad's angry outbursts were directed at Kirley and he simply came to expect it. Verbal abuse was the form of communication they shared and he was constantly reminded of the "stupid" disappointment he had become. To make up for his angry outbursts, Dad began taking him to the bars with him. Kirley had actually been drinking since he was nine years old. He would sneak cold beers from the fridge and often convince Dad to share a few "swigs" with him.

As the years passed, Kirley actually found unconditional love and total acceptance from Sherry. Yes, my shoplifting Christian friend. She had loved him for a long time and simply waited for his attention to turn her way. They decided to marry. Mom and I both tried to talk Sherry out of it. We knew she was signing up for heartache but she was convinced love would change him.

After they were married, he only became worse. He continued to drink and added to his addictions with several controlled substances. He would sell everything they owned to purchase the cheapest inhalants and then he would "huff" until he was totally incoherent. Together with his addicted friends, he would steal from anyone. He was never violent, he stole in secret. He would wait until Sherry was asleep or at work and then take anything he could to the pawn shop. He stole from Mom and Dad and even took their checkbooks and forged several hundred dollars woth of checks. Just to buy drugs.

While I was away on vacation one year, he broke into my house and stole several items. He took the stereo out of a car in my garage and sold it for drug money. My neighbors recognized him and said that he actually waved at them as he was loading up. I knew he had taken those things but I could not bring myself to confront him.

Things changed. Kirley and Sherry had two beautiful daughters. Because of his drug use it was extremely difficult for him to get a job. Sherry was forced to work to support the family, which fearfully left the girls at home in the care of their dad. He would never imagine harming those girls. He loved them more than life, just not more than drugs.

One night, the police discovered the girls, ages three and six at the time, alone in the dark house crying. They found Kirley out behind the house in a broken-down storage building, out of his mind from "huffing." They took the girls to Sherry's work and warned her they would remove the girls from the home through Child Protective Services if they ever found them in that condition again.

Everything came to a turning point one Thanksgiving Day. We were having dinner together with the entire family at Mom and Dad's. Sherry came into the room where I was and began to cry. She said she didn't know what to do anymore. Kirley's addiction had taken control of their lives and now the dealers were threatening her and the girls.

My first response was to pat her on the back and say, "I'll be praying." Then it hit me. The Bible says I'm a liar if I say I love my neighbor, pat them on the back, and say may it be well with you— when it is within my power to help.

I talked with Bubba regarding the situation and that night we took Sherry and the girls back to Tyler, TX, where we were living and hid them there from Kirley and the dealers.

Kirley was out of his mind worried about his family. After a few months we met with him and explained that we had taken them for their protection and that he could visit with them for a few hours. After his visit, he met with us and asked if we would help him turn his life around. He would move to Tyler and give up all drugs and alcohol.

With God's help, he did just that. Our church surrounded the entire family with loving support and helped to meet their needs until they were both employed and the restoration of their family was evident. Kirley's life became an example of the true miracle-working power of God. He was our trophy of grace!

His testimony was so unbelievable; many of his old friends could not even recognize him. Sadly, after only four years of living for God and making the right choices, Kirley died of cancer. His life was actually changed by love. What a wonderful end to a tragic story.

Jimmy

Jimmy and I were twins. Born three years after Kirley, he was the youngest son. His self-esteem issues were evident in his personality also. He was an entertainer much like Kirley. He was very good looking and with that, also extremely talented. He could charm almost anyone. He could morph his personality at the drop of a hat.

He was funny and friendly one moment and would become angry and aloof the next. He was the "Fonz." Happy Days was perfect for detailing exactly how a misfit could be cool by being bad. He had actually developed quite a following of girlfriends. He just couldn't find the key to acceptance with his peers. Eventually, his choices led him into trouble as well.

He internalized his feelings of inadequacy and maintained a strong outward appearance. Though he felt things strong and deep, he was careful not to let anyone in. The anger and desperation on the inside was reaching a boiling point and when he could no longer maintain a solid facade he began drinking heavily. Alcoholism separated him from every relationship of value to him.

He began to see himself as a failure and blamed Dad for his condition. Dad could see traces of himself in Jimmy and despised what he saw. Their mutual anger built huge walls between them and this created a lot of tension at family gatherings. He would usually leave early and angry.

He had established some friendships with several people at a local bar where he worked. You could find him there from open 'til close. He played the bass guitar and sang in the band some, until one night when he had been drinking excessively. The bar owner had actually taken his keys from him because he was much too intoxicated to drive.

Jimmy became very angry and grew physically violent. Rather than risk a physical altercation with him, his friend gave in and handed him the keys. Twelve minutes after he left the bar, Jimmy crashed into the side of an eighteen wheeler and died on impact. The tragic loss affected us all. Alcohol Kills.

Janice

Janice was the baby. She was an unexpected blessing. Born just thirteen months after the twins, she will always be known as the baby of the bunch. She was adored by all. Her beautiful complexion and pretty hair earned her attention from everyone. When people would look at our family they would always notice her. Maybe because she was the youngest, but I believe it was her beauty.

She withdrew as a young child. She found security hiding behind the rest of the kids. As she began to grow, she learned to adapt and actually began to shine. She was so cute to everyone that it became easy to act. She could appear as though she didn't have a care in the world.

Looking back now, I can see where she was starving for someone to see past her beauty to who she was on the inside. Just like the rest of us girls, she also longed to be loved and cared for.

She believed if she could find the love of a man she would be complete. Of course she could have had her pick of young men. After her first choice didn't work out, she found herself living as a single mother raising two children. Low self esteem causes us to question our ability to handle tough situations. She had to work hard to try and make it, but it was always evident that she was unsure and fearful.

Today she is married and has raised both of her children. Though she continues to struggle with self worth, she has proven to have survived the challenges with minimal damage.

In her own words: (Janice's E-mail)

"Well, I really had it a little easier than you guys. But I look back and remember I used to really pray when Dad would wake us up to clean house or just sing to him. But then the times that he yelled and smelled like a bottle of booze. I remember lying in the back of a station-wagon and saying to God, "Please get us to Grandma's." Daddy was driving drunk again. I guess after seeing my dad and my three brothers on the bottle was the most scary thing I remember about my childhood. Because Mom taught us to forgive, I did not like the fact that I had to forgive my dad and brothers. Because as a child I had hurt and anger. I wonder a lot where we would have been if there was no alcohol in our home as children. I really have to say that the effect of the alcohol in my childhood home really did not hit until I myself tasted alcohol at the age of 28 when I ran from a bad marriage. I was a single mom facing a large world with wonderful young children. I started to drink and have so much fun. But the honest fact is I came in one night and had a guy with me. He was going to say goodnight and leave but he did not, he decided to have his way with me. I would have screamed but my little six- year-old girl was knocking on my bedroom door wanting in at that time. All I could do was pull myself together after he stopped and go care for her. This was my wake-up call that I could become like the drinkers that I was raised with. I was so drunk I could not control the things around me or even control myself at the time. So I guess you can say since that day I have been so blessed to have had a mom that showed me the other side of my childhood. Which was trust in the Lord.

Judy, I hope this was what you were looking for. I have never had Mom's way with words. I hope it helps. I love you. Jan"

For several years during our teens, Jimmy, Janice, and I enjoyed the experience of singing with a small group of young people. We excelled in music, possibly because of the excessive amount of late night practices with Dad. His late night interruptions of our sleep paid off in at least one area. For us, it was the only light that shined in our dark lives.

If we found any opportunity for experiencing pride in ourselves, it would have been the moments spent on a church platform singing. Self esteem is increased when we get the chance to see ourselves as God sees us. Our worth is decided by the price He was willing to pay for us!

So much could be told of the lives lived out in our home, six different children with many of the same issues. The damaging effects of alcohol abuse continue to run deep in each generation of our family. It is what it is and we choose how we will survive. One common thread is that we love each other. Misery loves company.

January 4, 1977

I heard a new song on the radio today. I think I must have written it in some other life.

"I learned the truth at seventeen that love was meant for beauty queens and high school girls with clear skinned smiles who married young and then retired/

The valentines I never knew the Friday night charades of youth were spent on one more beautiful…. A brown eyed girl in hand-me-downs.

To those of us who knew the pain of valentines that never came/ And those whose names were never called when choosing sides for basketball/ It was long ago and far away/ The world was younger than today/ And dreams were all they gave for free/ To ugly duckling girls like me…

Yeah, that about sums it up for me. I'm destined to settle for seconds. I'm not the cheerleader, can't afford the uniforms and don't have the cute hair. I will never make the drill team, I can't afford drill camp and I haven't had any dance classes.

I am lucky; at least I can sing good enough to be in choir. Oh yeah, I guess it is an elective – really anyone can be in choir.

I'm seriously homely and I pretty much disappear in the halls. I wonder who decides which girls get to be pretty and which ones get to be smart. What would qualify me to have been chosen for rich and normal?

I do have a few friends but I'm not sure if they really like me as a person or if they simply feel sorry for me and I'm their good deed. Oh well, sometimes you just have to play with the hand you're dealt.

Can I pass this game?

P.S. Did I mention that I live at Dysfunction Junction?

APPLICATION

Self esteem is an extremely important part of our development. If our view of ourselves is well balanced, we can succeed in life. John Maxwell once said, "People go farther than they thought they could when someone else thinks they can." If there is a deficiency in our opinion of ourselves, we are almost always powerless to change on our own.

With God, all things are possible. As an adult, I began to sense the symptoms of a low self esteem were affecting many areas of my life. I realized that I had to surrender the feelings of inadequacy to God. He alone can change who I am. My past cannot define me and my future cannot overwhelm me if I am sure that He is in my present.

I could see that fear was having an effect on how I chose to approach a career. I wanted to believe I deserved the promotions, but I was afraid I would fail if I received one. I desired the ability to be assertive and confident but usually chose the least confrontational path.

Marriages fail because one or both of the parties involved are looking for completion in the other. We bring our dysfunctions with us into our relationships hoping one will cancel out the other. The problem is that our wholeness is only found in who we are in Christ.

Insecurity will undermine our ability to succeed in business. The inability to trust others immobilizes us and we cannot move into leadership positions. We become paralyzed by our own self doubt.

With God's help, I am continuing to rise above the damage caused by my lack of self esteem. I am discovering that I am God's creation, He didn't make another person quite like me and He has great plans for my life. Hope replaces doubt in my heart and I am expecting to be amazed with the outcome of my life.

- If diagnosed early, low self esteem can be overcome. It simply requires someone to be involved in another's life deeply enough to discover the issues. After that, an investment of quality time and kindness will go a long way toward pulling someone from the land of nobodies to the land of somebodies.

- Low self esteem causes the desperation of huge amounts of fear. The fear of inadequacy and mediocrity. Counseling can be a useful tool in moving people past the fear. Creating coping skills and developing the ability to see reality helps us see truth about who we really are.

- There is something to be said for focusing on self esteem development in a child. There are so many who are struggling because of circumstances beyond their control. When we get involved with self image restoration, we change the future and help overcome the past.

- God's Word offers a massive amount of encouragement. It reminds us that we are fearfully and wonderfully made. It reminds us that our God's thoughts of us are more than the sands of the seas. He loved us so much that He gave His only Son so that we could have hope and life.

You've heard the old saying, "It takes one to know one." Well, yes it's true. I can recognize someone struggling with low self esteem very easily. I am fully acquainted with the sense of nothingness and I have grown to despise its effects in the lives of those I love.

When I am speaking at a conference or mentoring one on one, I can share the truth of God's grace working in our lives. Because I know what it feels like, I have developed the ability to create word pictures that will help others see why they feel so unworthy. I came from a mighty long way!

Low self esteem is not only caused from growing up in a dysfunctional atmosphere, we can suffer its effects based on our own bad decisions. When we know we have made the wrong choices and are suffering the consequences it is so easy to just accept failure as our punishment.

Yes, we will reap what we sow. Yes, there will always be consequences for our behavior—but God, who is rich in mercy paid for our mistakes so that we could have life and that more abundantly. I know that sounds like I'm preaching but at least I'm preaching truth.

The purpose of God in my life was to utilize my experiences and struggles with self worth to help others understand His grace. The shame of sin in my life is a true testimony to His unfailing love and mercy. I'm sure I will never know every answer and I cannot change what I have lived through, but I am determined to offer all of it to Him for His use.

You are my hiding place...
You surround me with
songs of deliverance.
Psalm 32:7

BEYOND BROKEN

CIRCUMSTANCE

Pain has a purpose. I made the decision to write these pages filled with difficult experiences because I truly believe there was a specific purpose for everything. When I considered this chapter, I was faced with the greatest challenge. All forms of abuse are upsetting. Recovery from some circumstances is unattainable without the healing power of God.

The relationship that I shared with Steven, (my friend from the skating rink mentioned earlier) was close to unspeakable. The details are horrific and repulsive yet the value of the lesson learned is worth the risk of repulsion. Healing in this situation is a continual work in my heart and mind. Memories of violation are often the most difficult to overcome.

At the tender age of almost fourteen, a young girl struggling with self esteem issues can be extremely vulnerable. The desire for validation and the need to feel attractive can overwhelm reasoning and open the door for staggering exploitation. In my case the results were devastating.

I was excited about the opportunity to have a "first date" with Steven. I know, I was so young but I had been discussing it with Momma for weeks. I was already spending every moment at the skating rink with him, but he was almost 18 years old and she was concerned about our age difference.

I continually reminded her that I was the most mature of all of her children and she knew I had a good head on my shoulders. I would never do anything stupid. I know he was a little older but he really liked me and I so wanted to go on a date with him. After much pleading and reasoning, she gave in. My first date— the thought of it took my breath away. I could hardly sleep until Saturday night came.

When he pulled up in front of the house I knew what to expect. It was inevitable; Dad was drinking and insisted that he come in. I was sick to my stomach knowing how Dad was and realizing that Steven had no idea. I really didn't want him to see what the inside of the house looked like but I wasn't going to get to go if I didn't bring him in first.

He tried to be polite but I could tell right away he was extremely uncomfortable. Dad asked questions like, "Do you have a job or did you steal that car?" He explained that he worked in the family business, construction. "Do you attend school or did you drop out like out all the other punks around here?" His answer, "Well... I work too much, I quit school."

I tried to change the subject and hurry us out the door. "We have to go Dad, the movie will be starting in 20 minutes." On our way out the door we hear one last word from the porch, "She ain't on the pill yet son, take it easy!" Laughing from total embarrassment we headed out.

We grabbed a bite to eat then got onto the freeway. I was amazed at how fast his car would go. He was having fun showing off his driving ability and took one of the huge overpasses at over 100 miles per hour. I was terrified but he thought it was funny. Of course we didn't go to the movies but we drove around town. We got something cold to drink and ended up parking by one of the lakes nearby. I didn't mind at all. It was still so very exciting and I liked to kiss. I had already made it very clear to Steven that I had no intentions of going any farther physically because I was a Christian girl and I was waiting until marriage to have sex.

He laughed and whined a little but agreed to honor my request until I changed my mind. How wonderful. He really cared for me enough to wait. I was home by 11:00 p.m. as agreed and I struggled to fall asleep from all of the excitement. That, and Dad was getting loud again in the other room. He was questioning why mom ever decided to let me go out with a boy as young as I was.

She defended me until the argument was futile and she went on to bed herself. My older sister Kathy whispered across the bedroom, "I can't believe she let you go out at fourteen, I had to wait till I was sixteen!" We laughed and went off to sleep.

As time passed, our relationship became more dependent. If I wasn't with him I was on the phone with him. I did not realize the web of control he was building around me, I didn't care. I liked having someone who cared for me and openly claimed me as his own . Eventually, the relationship began to take a downward spiral. He was becoming more aggravated that I would not have sex with him and I was feeling the desperation of holding on to him.

He called one night and advised me that he was going to have sex with an old friend of his. If I wasn't going to meet his needs then I should at least allow him to spend the night with her. Wait, what? Why would he do that? He loves me. His reply, "This had nothing to do with love." It was just sex and she was okay with it.

A few days later, he picked me up to go skating. We headed in the direction of the skating rink but he turned down a different street. I asked, "Where we are going?" He said "I want you to see where I live." I thought this was a wonderful idea; I would get to meet his parents. This must mean that he loved me and wanted their approval.

We pulled up in front of a beautiful home. It was large and the entrance was groomed well. The driveway was long and led up to a pathway that curved toward the door. I was taken by surprise. I knew he had enough money to go out and have fun, but I never expected him to live in this neighborhood. Wow. The house wasn't brand new but it was much newer than the one I lived in. He laughed at my response to his home.

We walked into the living room area and I kept looking around for his mother. I asked quietly, "Where are your parents?" He laughed again, "Oh, they're out of town." I was relieved and disappointed at the same time. "We shouldn't be here then." I remember thinking we needed to leave but he insisted we sit on the couch and talk.

I was old enough to know that I didn't need to put myself in that situation, but I was young enough and insecure enough to give in to his wishes. I just didn't want to go all the way. We could "make out" on the couch but please, that's all I want to do.

"Don't worry. I know." From that moment, he became another person. It did not matter what I was saying, he wasn't listening and I could not stop him. He was much stronger and more determined than I was. My thoughts raced through every scenario. Okay, I've done it this time. I shouldn't have put myself in this position. It's all my fault and I know it. This is it Judy, just deal with it. That evening was not at all what my little girl mind expected it to be. I had dreams of a beautiful place and a tender young man whose desire was to love me forever.

When I arrived home that evening, I went directly to my room. I had cried all the way home and I didn't want my mom to see my eyes. She called out to me but I told her I was so tired I just wanted to go to sleep. It was dark in the room so when she glanced in the door she couldn't tell.

Lying there in the dark, my mind was racing. My heart was devastated and I was experiencing pain from the forceful way he had handled me. At that moment, I felt so alone. There was not a person breathing that I could talk to. I couldn't bear the thought that someone would know what I had done and I couldn't bear it if I was not allowed to see him again.

He would be the man I would marry. You are only supposed to have sex with one man and so that night the decision was made in my mind. I'll just marry him when I finish school and this will all be okay. It's amazing what we can rationalize in our messed up thought processes.

After that night, he became much more controlling. He was extremely jealous and now that he had control of me physically, I belonged to him. He became physically abusive, hitting me and pinching my arms and legs if I even saw another guy walk by. He was so angry one night because I spoke to a neighbor that he took his cigarette and held it to my arm. Burning me and laughing at the same time.

I continued to hide the abuse from everyone because I had made up my mind we would be married. We were having sex, so we would be married. The abuse became even more appalling. He operated somewhere between barely normal and distorted perversion. I still don't know what he was thinking and how any of his actions could bring him such pleasure.

He spent time thinking up ways to torment me. He took me out into a huge wooded area close to the lake where he lived. He insisted I take all of my clothes off and close my eyes. He had a surprise for me. I asked him not to make me do this but he became forceful and left me no choice. I closed my eyes in fear of what would happen next.

I could hear the sounds of leaves and sticks breaking but I wasn't sure what was going on. After a few minutes, I opened my eyes to discover that he had taken my clothes and left me there alone and naked. Why? I called out to him and cried, "Please don't do this to me, Steven. Please come back." I could hear him laughing in the distance.

It was fall and the breeze was causing a chill. While I was sitting on the ground fearful, ashamed, and disgusted I thought for the first time, maybe I should end this relationship. So what if he was the first, I can find someone else who will forgive me. The fear of his response held me captive for many more months. I was furious with him but at the same time I knew if I reacted too much he would hurt me. After about thirty minutes, which felt like thirty hours, he returned and brought my clothes.

Steven got an apartment with some of his friends. They shared the expenses and girlfriends. I refused to participate in that exchange, however I suffered many hours of sexual, physical, and emotional abuse in that little place. I hated pulling up in the parking lot because I knew what was coming next. Still today, I cringe when I drive by that area. I expect them to condemn that place any day now. I think I will show up for the demolition and light a candle.

He was very good at carrying on an appearance of normalcy. Everyone thought we were just like all the other teenagers. Sure, we appeared to be fussing every once in a while but didn't everyone do that? I had to work more diligently at hiding the bruises and I had to put on a mask to protect Mom from ever finding out. It would crush her heart and I couldn't bear causing her that pain.

I do find it interesting that this horrendous abuse was carried out over the space of several months and no one noticed. No one saw the devastation taking place. I was losing me in the cruel, secret agony of living. Did others see? Or did they simply turn and look the other way? School teachers, friends, no one in our neighborhood, not even the church. Why?

Honestly, where were the women in the church? Could they not see something was seriously going wrong in my life? The Sunday School teachers or the Youth workers, anyone?

One night he was unusually evil. He crossed the line and did things I cannot put into words. I'm not sure I could adequately provide the words to describe his actions. I cannot imagine anything more vile and cruel could be acted upon by someone who insists they love you. Something inside snapped and I fought back. I ran as hard as I could to get away and when I finally made it home I was hysterical.

I could never tell Momma the truth so I just told her that we broke up. She said she was glad because she just didn't like the way he was treating me. God was merciful to protect her from the entire story. Steven didn't give up that easy. He liked having full control of another person so he would call and beg and plead with me to come back to him. I felt sorry for him because he would cry and insist how sorry he was and that he couldn't live without me. He needed me.

He would show up at my school and drive around the campus over and over revving up his engine and letting me know he was there. I would go out to his car after school and tell him I was sorry. I told him I still loved him but my Mother would call the police on him if she knew I was talking to him.

I agreed to meet him at the skating rink and talk it over the next weekend. I waited outside for him to pull in. When he did, I walked over to his car window and told him that it had to be over. I needed him to leave me alone and let me go on with my life. That's when he reached over to his glove compartment and pulled out a gun.

I could not believe it. I was so angry at him. Why would he dare threaten me with a gun? His answer, "It's not for you, it's for me." He held the gun to his head and began to cry. He said, " I cannot live without you. I would rather be dead."

I began to cry and beg him to put the gun away. The panic I was experiencing at that moment caused my heart to race and I felt as though I would faint. Fear was overwhelming my thought processes and I began to shake.

I was pleading with him to forgive me and I told him I would try to find a way that we could be together again. Then, he began to laugh hysterically. I was stunned. Why was he laughing? What was he thinking? He threw the gun against the passenger door and hit the gas pedal. He burned out and left a trail of rubber for at least a block. The smoke from his exhaust hadn't cleared before my mother pulled back into the skating rink. She saw me outside and said she had a feeling something was wrong and had to come back to the rink.

She called the police and placed a restraining order on Steven. She would not allow me to answer the phone at home for weeks. He would call and beg her to let him speak to me. The police watched the school and when he discovered they were there, he never came back.

Almost two weeks later, one of his friends called my home and asked to speak to me. Mom wasn't home so I took the call. He said he just wanted to let me know that Steven had gotten drunk over the weekend and married one of the girls he had been sleeping with. Two weeks before, he would have killed himself for me and now he was married to someone else.

For months, I walked through a very dark emotional place. I couldn't bear to eat. I had no desire to speak; I was exhausted from the physical torment and emotionally ravaged . The ache in my heart would not let up and I wanted to die. No one could reach inside and fix all of the broken areas. I thought no one would ever want to.

My family simply assumed I was recovering from a broken heart. They had no idea I was simply broken. I existed in a zombie-like state for several months. I was an empty shell trying to survive until I could feel again. I needed counseling but there was so much chaos happening in my home that no one even noticed.

I developed my own defense mechanism. I told myself, "If I just won't think about it, it will go away." Not thinking is really easy for a zombie. The devastation I suffered during that season of my life affected me for eternity.

Steven will not take anything else away from me. The savage attack on my innocence and my faith has only served to make me wiser and more effective at discernment.

November 10, 1977

I don't think I can do this. How did I come to this place in my life? I can't even speak. No one would ever believe me. No one would ever understand how I got myself into this.

Holy Crap

I hate him. I hate him. I love him. I hate him. I don't even know anymore. It doesn't matter anyway, he's gone.

Why did this happen? Where is God? I'm hurting so bad and I can't even explain why. My head hurts so bad. My stomach hurts. I don't want to live without him. I don't want to see him ever again.

I'm so confused. He said he loved me but he makes me sick. I will never love anyone like I loved him. I will never love anyone again. It hurts too much.

I don't know how to go on and I don't know how to go back. I'm so confused. I'm so sick. It hurts so bad!

I need to escape from life.

"Date rape" and abuse are much more prevalent in our society than we would like to admit. Because sexual promiscuity has become widely accepted as the norm, we have lost our ability to separate yes from no.

Young people are experimenting with sex at much younger ages. We try to take steps to protect them from the consequences of their choices. Birth control pills and condoms will never protect the hearts and minds that are being ravaged on a daily basis. The emotional damage inflicted by the exchange of innocence in the pursuit of love is devastating our society.

A common characteristic of unhealthy and abusive relationships is the control that the abusive partner seeks to maintain. Parents are rarely aware of such controlling tactics as these appear to be merely relational issues.

"Date Rape" is actually a term that has been used to describe forced or coerced sexual acts between; partners, dates, friends, or acquaintances, performed against the will of another or without consent. ⅔ Two-thirds of rapists are known to the victim, yet ninety-seven percent of them never spend a day in jail. Most victims tend to blame themselves for having been with the person by choice. They feel guilty, dirty, and scared.

Healthy relationships should remain free from violence and fear. Parents can protect their teens from abusive situations by standing up for them—-even if it means going against their wishes. Young people mature at different levels, but they have one thing in common, they need to be protected. They have friends, what they need is a parent to be observant and determined.

Familiarize yourself with some of the warning signals of an abusive relationship involving young people:

- Unexplained injuries or bruises

- Loss of interest in usual activities

- Nervous laughter to cover anxiety

- Increasingly isolated

Rape or abusive actions perpetrated by someone who is known or trusted will cause teens to be less likely to seek crisis services, tell someone, report to police, or seek counseling. The actions carry significant psychological effects.

Victims often have issues with believing they deserved to be raped, especially if they agreed to go to a date's house, room, or car. The truth is that no one deserves to be raped. The choice to spend time with a person is not an open agreement for sexual activity.

Consider these facts when discussing rape issues with young women:

- If you don't want to have sex, say "NO" loud, like you mean it and fight it off if you have to.

- If you have been raped, or possibly drugged and raped, get to the emergency room as soon as possible for a rape kit exam.

- Call a rape crisis hotline to talk with a professional counselor. National Hotline is 800-799-SAFE.

- Get ongoing counseling to deal with the trauma.

There is a silent hopelessness that comes from hiding the pain and shame of an abusive relationship. After a while you feel trapped in your present situation and give up on ever finding the escape route. The need for others around you to be proactive at intervention is great. Getting involved at the right time can make the difference between life and death.

Recovery is a process. Surviving atrocious, evil abuse at the hands of someone you love has long term repercussions. I've wondered how it could be that I would have experienced such hideous cruelty and violence without purpose. I mean, really? How could this ever be used for good in my life?

I refused to allow the devastation of abuse to steal my future. I would not allow my memories of the past to keep me from the joy of making memories for years to come. God knew that I would be in a place to utilize every moment of torment as an example of His ability to restore the broken.

I can more clearly describe how much He loves me by understanding what it is to love someone who intentionally harms you. Even in my young mind, I discovered ways to hold on to what I knew of God long enough to maintain my sanity.

His continual mercy will never make sense to me. How He saw my choices and heard my heart cry out in desperate shame because of those choices. I choose to share these terrifying moments with very few. I try to be sensitive to the direction of God and utilize truth regarding this time in my life to offer hope in desperation.

May I be honest? God is still working on the restoration process of my mind and emotions. I am truly living everyday by faith and allowing His purposes to be revealed in me. I do remain fully convinced that, "He who began a good work in me will be faithful to complete it!"

Ask where the good way is...
and walk in it.
Jeremiah 6:16

BLIND LEADING BLIND

CIRCUMSTANCE

It's the sick, weak sheep that get disconnected from the fold and are attacked and wounded. I remember hearing a preacher describe the danger of separation from a church fold using that statement. It makes sense. The sheep is ignorant. All sheep are considered to be dumb. They wander off—-away from the other sheep and don't even notice they are alone until the wolf comes and attacks them.

I guess you could have considered me a dumb sheep that had been viciously attacked after ignorantly wandering off. I was never out of the sight of the Shepherd. He saw me. I had actually been hiding in the middle of the other sheep, bleeding to death and none of the other dumb sheep even noticed.

Well, until one day. The second biggest mistake I ever made walked into my life. We'll call this a relationship with Matthew. He was a wonderful, talented, outgoing, and friendly youth sponsor at our church. He was married to a pretty wife and they had everything going for them. A great family, good friends and a promising future with a picture-perfect life.

I was continuing to recover from the devastation of Steven when Matthew and his sweet wife, Jill, noticed for the first time that I was hurting. They began to reach out to me and try to help me to come out of the depression I was obviously struggling with. They did not know anything about what I had just come through.

They did know that my home life was stressful and miserable and assumed my actions were because of it. They felt sorry for me and my brothers and sisters and tried to help us become more active in our youth group. They would plan activities that we could participate in and even give us a ride when needed.

Eventually, I began to trust them and enjoyed spending time with them. They were older and much more interesting than anyone I had been involved with before. The laughter I experienced around them was rare and in a strange way began to bring some relief to the dark heaviness in my mind.

Until one evening after a service at church. Matthew had offered to give us a ride home. When we pulled into the driveway, my family went on in and I remained outside visiting with Matthew and one of his friends. We were joking around about something and it felt different. It made me a little uncomfortable so I dismissed myself and went on in.

That night I struggled with my emotions. I was aware of the fact that I was much more "experienced" than most of the other girls in the youth group. I felt as though I wasn't as pretty or as well dressed as them but I knew things they didn't. I wondered if the older guys, even the men like Matthew could see the difference. I began to think of it as something that made me "special." I liked the attention I was receiving from him and a part of me wanted more.

At the age of almost fifteen, I had already lived through more than most but I was very young and in an extremely vulnerable state of mind. I liked the feeling of forgetting the pain and I seemed to feel that way whenever he was around. So I made every effort to be where he was.

He began to notice my interest in him and it became something he enjoyed. It was as though he desired my attention and would create opportunities to be where I was. The thrill of the moment was overtaking the sadness of the past and I was beginning to come alive again. That's what Momma thought and she loved it.

She was so thankful that Matthew and his wife had taken such an interest in me and she was amazed at how much better I was doing. The relationship she was so thankful for was a deception in the highest form. We began to flirt and tease each other with words that others couldn't hear.

The excitement of a "married man" taking an interest in me confused and thrilled me at the same time. Secret sin has an adrenaline factor that overtakes your senses and destroys your ability to reason. I'm not saying it was all Matthew. I enjoyed the ride so I paid for the gas. I didn't run when I should have and he didn't back away when he should have.

I knew he was taking advantage of me and I didn't care. I believed it was a temporary game that I was willing to play because it relieved my pain. He was not at all innocent. He enjoyed the game enough to take it to the next level as he began to plan for much more intimate experiences.

The fun lasted for weeks and I never realized what was happening to me until it was too late. Matthew was twenty-three and I was barely fifteen. He was old enough to know better and I was young enough not to care. The youth group was growing and everyone thought he and Jill were doing such a great job helping out in that department. They were not the youth leaders, only sponsors but the kids liked them so well.

Jill had to work a lot and Matthew was finishing up his classes at a nearby community college. This allowed him to have a lot of free time on his hands. Over time, the relationship developed into a fulltime affair. I knew it was wrong but I felt like I needed someone and he was willing to be there for me.

He knew it was wrong but he was beginning to get all mixed up between the physical and emotional attraction. As time passed, the "excitement" began to wear off for me. I didn't like that I was in another relationship that was leading me nowhere fast. I told him I wanted to break it off but he would not even discuss it.

By this time, he said he knew it was wrong but he couldn't help it. He had feelings for me and didn't want to end it just yet. Once again, I was flattered by the thought of someone desiring me and so I continued to play along. Until the day Jill made a huge announcement to our youth group. She and Matthew would be having their first baby.

What was I thinking? What a wake-up call. I disguised my stunned shock with a huge smile and shared in the offering of congratulations. I headed out of the church to try to hide somewhere and breathe for a minute. I hardly had time to reason with myself before Matthew found me and pleaded with me not to leave him.

I couldn't even talk. I just wanted him to leave me alone. That was the first time he threatened to make a huge scene and tell everyone the whole truth. The thought of everyone finding out totally alarmed me. There was no way I could bear for Jill to be hurt by my actions. She was so good to me and she loved me sincerely. More than anyone in the church ever had.

I could never bring that level of shame to my momma. She had lived through so much; this would send her to her grave. I insisted he say nothing and I promised to stay with him. My emotions shut down again that day. How could anyone love me and plan a future with someone else? Once again, I tried to understand the love of a man and it fell short.

For almost five years Matthew held me in the cage of his control. He utilized his threats to keep me under his domination. I was at his complete mercy. As long as I followed his instructions, he was good to me. He continued to insist that he loved me on a deep level. He just couldn't leave his kids. He loved Jill, I knew that. I loved her too—too much to hurt her heart with the truth of our betrayal.

Yes, he had his cake and ate it too. Of course my mom continued to support our "church" relationship because she believed it was helping me. She had no idea that church was just the right cover for a very wrong connection.

The control became increasingly stronger. I was to answer the phone at a certain time each morning and each night. I was to meet him wherever he said even if it meant skipping school. I was not allowed to talk with the boys at church and certainly no one at school. I was not allowed to attend the prom or any other function that required a date.

My friends and family felt sorry for me and could not understand why I didn't seem interested in anyone. My Mom had a serious discussion with me. She insisted it was not normal for any girl my age not to be going out with boys. I assured her it was just that I hadn't found the right one yet.

If I was not where I was supposed to be at all times, Matthew became angry to the point of violence. He was utilizing fear to manipulate my world. He knew I loved others too much to harm them with the truth so the truth became his weapon.

As time passed, I became increasingly unhappy with no promise of a future and absolutely no joy in the present. I had turned off my feelings for him because feelings were too hard to endure. "If I don't think about it – it doesn't matter," became my life's motto. I was simply surviving one day at a time without thinking.

One day, Jill came to my work and shared with me that she was concerned about my feelings for Matthew. She was worried that we had become too close and wanted me to back away from him. I was crucified. I told her she was wrong and that I had no feelings for him. I'm sure she didn't believe me because from that day on she began to distance herself from me.

Every church function became the place where I would receive my instructions for the next day. Every day was filled with trying to cover up for the lies and deception required to continue the relationship. I became overwhelmed with the pressure of it and finally decided to begin doing what I wanted. I had a friend who was part of a youth group at another church. I had been told that he was interested in going out with me so I let his friend know that I was interested.

We'll call him John. He visited our church one Sunday night and saved a place beside him for me to sit. After I sang in the service, I left the platform and went to sit down beside him.

I remember thinking, What was Matthew going to do? Make a scene in the middle of service? Surely, he's not that crazy. I was wrong. He acted like he had a message for me and he walked right up the aisle into the pew behind us. He leaned over and pinched my neck extremely hard and told me to get up and leave.

I couldn't believe it. What choice did I have? I waited a minute until I heard him clear his throat behind me. In submission, I whispered I was getting ill and I left. I got in my car and left before Matthew could get out to the parking lot. I was stunned by his boldness and now more fearful than ever. I was also more angry than ever.

John called me the next day and we made arrangements to meet. I could not allow him to come to where I lived because we would get caught. How sad it was for a perfectly normal date to be something I was afraid of being caught on?

I really enjoyed being with him and I'm sure that relationship could have been something good for my life but it was ended before it could develop.

That night when I returned home, Matthew was waiting at the end of my street. When I saw him I knew I was in trouble. I pulled over, parked my car, and got into the car with him. He drove a few streets over and exploded. He pulled my arm behind my back and demanded I tell him where I was and who I was with.

I told him I was upset about our relationship and that I needed to think. I said I had been driving around to clear my mind and I was on my way home to call him.

He was out of his mind with anger. I realized that night that he could be extremely dangerous. For the first time I was seriously concerned for my life. I kept asking myself, How did I come to this? Why is my life so screwed up?

I really wanted out. I couldn't stand this any longer. I simply continued putting it out of my mind. "If I don't think about it, it won't matter." That night as I was trying to go to sleep I broke down and began crying out to God. I asked Him to help me find a way out. I told Him I was so lonely and I just wanted to know there was someone He had created for me.

I fell asleep crying. I am convinced that God gave me a specific dream that night and I will never forget it. I was part of a singing group at church and I really enjoyed it. In my dream, I was up on the platform singing and I saw young guy with blonde hair enter the sanctuary and walk across the back area. He caught my eye but I couldn't make out who he was.

When I woke up, I remembered the dream and the feeling I experienced as I watched this guy walk in. I believed God had tried to show me that He does have a plan and He was going to bring it to pass.

I felt a strange calm about it. Things didn't change immediately. I was still under Matthew's full control but I kept my eyes open for an escape. During this period of time a young kid who had been playing drums for our church singing group began joking around with some of the guys about wanting to take me out.

The other kids made jokes about it because everyone was convinced I wouldn't go out with anyone. I was waiting for "Mr. Perfect." I was. He began to tease with me about going out with him. He was actually three years younger than me and I joked back with him saying, "I don't babysit!" We were good friends and I liked it that way. We all called him "Bubba," that's what his mother called him and we all thought it was so cute. He was like a little brother.

He backed off for a while and I didn't give it a second thought. I was not going to get him in trouble with Matthew. I knew it was much too dangerous to give him any reason to hurt anyone else.

One night after church, we were all sitting around talking and "Bubba" called me over to where he was. Matthew was in another room so I figured it was safe enough. I sat down across from where he was and a few others gathered around. He had learned to play a song on the guitar and he wanted to show it to me.

He was so cute. He was singing and watching his finger placement on the guitar. He never looked up as he sang, "If a picture paints a thousand words, then why can't I paint you..." As I sat there watching him, I thought to myself, Wow, he is really cute, if I'm not careful I could actually have feelings for this kid. I told him he did a good job and went back to my controlled zone for everyone's safety.

I could never be, say, or do what I wanted. Matthew had a code he would use if I was doing something I shouldn't. If I let my guard down and enjoyed myself, if I laughed too loud or became the center of attention he would simply say, "I like vanilla ice cream." That meant I was not to be noticed, he didn't want others enjoying who I was because he didn't want to share me.

The emotional and mental control was taking its toll on me. I began researching places that I could run to. I was out of high school now and I could start a new life in another city, if I could think of a way to do it so that I couldn't be found. I was too worried it would hurt my momma. I loved her so much and she was suffering through so many things with all my brothers and sisters, not to mention dealing with my dad.

One night we were at the church and service was going to begin in a few moments. I looked back for just a second and lost my breath. There he was, walking in the door and across the back of the sanctuary. It was Bubba. The one I dreamed of was Bubba!

I was startled back to reality when Matthew pinched my arm real hard and asked what I was looking at. I told him I was trying to remember something and I promised I wasn't looking at anything specific. He saw Bubba with a group of other guys at the back but he didn't figure it out yet.

A few months later, on a Wednesday night before Thanksgiving, Matthew and Jill were out of town. I was at church as usual and Bubba was hanging around after service. We were all laughing and joking when he gathered up the nerve once more to ask me out.

I told him I would meet him down the street at a McDonald's but he could never tell anyone. He agreed and we met up secretly later that night. I'm not sure what it was other than providence, but I believe that was the night I knew I loved him. It was one of my favorite and only pleasant memories of youth.

Time passed and reality sat back in. Matthew returned and in a few weeks he had noticed Bubba's interest in me. I had assured him there was nothing there and that he was way too young but he insisted something was up and threatened me if I talked to him at all.

Bubba couldn't figure it all out yet. He thought I wanted him but I was sending him mixed signals. He asked me why was it that he felt like he was reaching out his hand to me and I would almost take it and then push it away. I had to push him away for his own good. After a few weeks he moved on and began going out with another girl at church. I thought I would die. Here I was again, missing life. I was dying on the inside and no one could help me.

I would fall onto the altar at the close of every service. I was begging God to help me or let me die. I couldn't go on. I was heartsick. I knew I was supposed to be with Bubba but I couldn't risk hurting everyone else in my life that I loved.

If Matthew followed through with his threats to tell everyone, I would be the reason for destroying so many people in the church. What shame it would bring to Jill and her children. How devastated my momma would be. And what if he really did hurt Bubba? I would just die! Why couldn't I just die?

I was consumed with thoughts of Bubba. I would drive by his house on the way home from church just for the chance to see his car. Hoping he would be home and not out with someone else. I couldn't bear feeling like this.

Finally, I was on my way home one night after driving by his house. When I turned on the main road off of his street, I saw a car racing up behind me. I pulled over to get out of the way when I recognized the car. It was Matthew. Out of fear I pulled over and stopped my car in the far right lane.

He was a madman. He jumped out of his car, ran over to my car and pulled the door open. He began hitting me over and over again asking me, "What do you think you're doing? "Why are you doing this?" He was out of control, again.

I began to cry out of fear and I kept telling him, "I'm sorry, please stop!" He finally came to himself and began crying and saying, "I'm sorry." For the second time in my life, something on the inside snapped and I became a different person. I waited until he was calm and we agreed to talk about it the next day. He was late getting home and I was hurting too much to talk.

October 7, 1980

Dear God,

Who decides the level of brokenness that one person can handle? I know sin causes death. My sin has caused me to want to die but I can't. How is that fair? What did I do to deserve this level of pain? I need your help. I want out of this situation, I just don't know how. You know that I love you, I hate doing this. I don't want to be like this. I want to live for you with all my heart and stop hiding behind lies. I can't bear the thought that my actions are going to destroy so many people.

How can I tell Bubba the truth? He will never love me then. How can I tell Jill the truth? It will destroy her. How can I tell Momma the truth? Hasn't she had enough to deal with? What about the rest of my family? What about the church?

Please help me figure this out. I need an escape. I need an answer. I just want out…

Inappropriate relationships in the church are nothing new. One of the most damaging attacks against the church comes when the trust of leadership is broken. When the relationship between the followers and the leaders is compromised, everyone loses.

Risk management directors for church organizations across America are finding themselves forced to put policies into effect that will protect the foundation of the body from legal destruction. This action is based on the challenges facing churches of every size and denomination, all because of the vast amount of illicit affairs in churches.

I call it, "The Blind leading the Blind," because that's what it is. We have broken people trying to lead broken people. Pastors, teachers, deacons and volunteer sponsors are not exempt from human failure. However, the amount of damage their failure can afford should be limited.

The victims may not be innocent, but if they are under age they should be protected by the church. It is vitally important that safeguards and checkpoints are put into place to ensure the safekeeping of the hearts and lives of all involved.

Some suggested guidelines:

We are instructed to, "Know them that labor among us.". Complete applications with references and background information should be on file for every person who will come in contact with anyone under 18 years of age—Paid staff or volunteer. References should be followed up on.

Legal background checks should be made on every person who will come in contact with anyone under the age of 18. This includes all volunteers in every area of ministry or service. These records should be updated every two years.

Complete safety training and policy and procedures should be covered in depth during orientation and training of all staff and volunteers.

Access to all areas of the church facilities should be given to very few. There should never be an opportunity for a violation to occur. Safeguards should be put in place that would not allow for a male and female to be alone in a secluded area. Windows and doors should allow for visibility at all times.

Staff training should include warnings and signals of inappropriate action. Every leader should have an eye trained to see danger and a heart sensitive to discernment and revealed truth.

Blind trust of any staff member sets up an open door for failure. Every person in leadership should be in an accountable relationship with another leader. When we know each other's weaknesses, we can protect each other.

Counsel, prayer, and guidance of young people should never take place one-on-one. There should always be at least two adults present.

Transport of underage youth should always involve more than one person in the car at the same time. Drivers should be aware of their locations and drop off members of the opposite sex first.

In today's culture, deception does not only involve male and female relationships. More churches are also discovering the risk of inappropriate relationships developing between people of the same gender.

If we are wise, we will take every precaution to prevent the opportunity for devastation. You cannot be too safe. There is a plan to destroy your church. Don't be a part of it.

Control and manipulation are serious strongholds. When caught in the web, the more you fight against it the more entangled you become. Looking back now, I have come to the understanding that I survived for a purpose. I am extremely passionate about guarding relationships in the church.

Every level of ministry is vulnerable to the devices of the enemy. I now serve as co-pastor on staff at a church and assist in overseeing three other ministries. I consider myself a "watchdog". I understand and recognize red flags others may never see.

Having lived through it, I know all the tricks of deception. I sense and feel things on a much deeper level. I don't have a problem calling things into question and changing policies to prevent inappropriate actions.

I have a strong gift of discernment and am sensitive to any red flags. I have no shame in watching closely and listening intently. If I can take one step to prevent what I experienced from happening to anyone else, I will, without apology.

God can use anything we experience to teach others the risks involved. I know I broke His heart during those years of shame, but I intend to turn it around and use it as a tool of protection for every church I can reach.

I have been given the opportunity to speak to church staffs and share my story with groups of leaders who need to know the warning signs. It's amazing to watch as the light comes on in their eyes when I describe the simple things that can be done to prevent tragedies of fraud and abuse.

God will never change your past, but He can use the mistakes of your past to warn others.

You have turned my
mourning into dancing...
Psalm 30

KNIGHT-TIME OR NIGHT-TIME?

CIRCUMSTANCE

Sometimes, you just have to look at where you are and decide if it's worth staying there. Are you content with life as it is, or do you have what it takes to make a change? I came to the place where the pain of staying the same was much greater than the pain of change. I didn't know exactly how to get out of the relationship with Matthew but I knew I wanted out. I knew I wanted to be with Bubba and I was willing to risk it all if necessary. So, I decided to begin by telling Bubba the truth. I made plans to meet with him in a safe place close to a city park.

I began to explain to him that I had made some wrong decisions and was now in a relationship with Matthew. I explained that the power he used to control me was the threat of telling the truth. The truth would hurt so many people, but I had come to the point that I wanted to be with him so much, I was willing to stand up and face the truth.

If after knowing the truth he still wanted to be with me, I had plans to go and talk with the pastor of our church and confess. After that, I wasn't sure where to go. I was thinking I would ask the pastor to help me. Bubba explained that he had suspected the relationship with Matthew for a long time but just didn't know that I wanted out. I told him I was worried he would get hurt. He acted as though he was okay with the truth. I believed he was still interested in having a relationship with me. I felt the anxiety of moving forward and the excitement of hope waking up in my heart again.

I contacted the pastor and asked to meet with him. He agreed and we met at a local restaurant. As I began to explain from the beginning what was going on, the pastor looked at me and admitted that he knew it had been going on for a while. I asked why he hadn't said anything. His answer, "Let him who is without sin cast the first stone." I discovered later, the Pastor was involved in an affair himself.

He made plans with me to meet with Matthew and Jill after service the next week. I tried to act as though everything was "normal" until immediately following service. I went directly to his office to wait for the meeting to begin. I remember the fear that gripped my heart as I played every scenario possible over and over in my head. I was sick.

As Matthew and Jill came in with the pastor and found a seat, I could feel the heat of his eyes burning into me. Jill started to say something but he put his hand on her and told her not to say anything. The pastor closed the door and began to speak. He explained that I had come to him and shared that I wanted the freedom to begin seeing Bubba and that I believed Matthew was not going to allow me to do that because he and I had been involved in an inappropriate relationship.

The room was silent for a few seconds then Jill looked at Matthew and asked, "Is it true?" He didn't answer; he just continued to stare right at me with disbelief. I stared at the ground as tears began to burn in my eyes. I was finally on the edge of escape and I was terrified.

The pastor asked him, "Do you have anything to say?" He said, "I don't care what she does." That's when I looked up at him. Then Jill asked me, "Is it true?" I looked back down to the ground and shook my head, yes. I could not bear to look at her. I felt like I was the lowest of the low and I harmed someone I loved so much. She was not deserving of any of this.

Then the pastor said, "Judy wants you to leave her alone and let her go on with the rest of her life. I think that would be best for everyone involved, don't you?" Matthew didn't answer. He began to cry. I was so afraid he was getting ready to explode again. I didn't know what to do or say at this point.

Jill began to cry and she asked Matthew why he was doing this. She asked him if he would leave me alone. He was angry at this point and he snapped back, "If that's what she wants, fine!" Jill looked at me and said, "Is that what you want?" I gathered enough nerve to hold my head up and look at him then over to her. Our eyes met for the first time in the meeting and I began to cry. I said, "Yes, I'm so sorry". She looked at him and then said to the Pastor, "We need to leave now". He said nothing; he tightened his lip and nodded his head. Matthew grabbed his keys from the desktop and bumped into my shoulder on his way out the door. Jill followed behind him.

My shoulders dropped and I began to fall apart. The pastor walked over to offer me comfort. I looked at him with broken anger rising up in my heart and I asked why he didn't protect me from this. His answer, "I didn't know how."

I wish I could say a load was lifted off of me that day, but honestly, I never felt worse in all my life. I felt lower than the woman who was thrown at Jesus feet after being caught in the act of adultery. I was that woman; I deserved to be stoned for my choices. I would have felt better if I could have paid for my sin.

Actually, I had paid for my sin day after day for several years. That didn't help Jill. Now, she had to live with the effect of my sin and she was the innocent one. If the truth was announced from the mountain top, everyone I loved would pay for my sin. I wanted to die, again.

The pastor explained that he was going to try to keep this between us so that others wouldn't have to be drawn into it. I nodded as I walked out of his office.

Bubba was waiting to make sure I was ok. I had done it, I wasn't sure if it was actually done yet. I think I was still in shock.

That night when I went to bed, I fell apart. I had the strangest emotions. I wanted God to forgive me and for the first time since I was a little girl, I wanted my daddy to hold me. I needed the protection and the comfort of a father.

I was exhausted. I slept for two days straight. I was fearful the first few days after the meeting that Matthew would find me and try to talk to me but I was thankful it was finally over. He didn't contact me and I was relieved.

Now I could begin my relationship with Bubba with no fear of trouble. I was twenty years old now and I had already experienced so much heartache that I was starving for a good, healthy, normal love relationship.

I knew he was younger than me, but he was so mature in some ways it was hard to believe he was so young. I wanted to be where he was every minute of the day. He called me first thing when he woke up in the mornings and I would be the last call he made when he went to sleep at night. I was a different person when he was around. I held onto him for life.

Not long after we began spending all our time together, our friends and family began to warn us that our relationship was moving too fast. They thought we should take some time because of our age difference and because we weren't ready for a committed relationship.

He had become my knight in shining armor. He had rescued me from years of captivity and I was his damsel in distress. Our relationship was intoxicating. I found in him everything I had missed out on, and he found in me a princess who desperately needed to be protected and cared for.

We were two broken people who only felt complete when we were together. One night, I was walking out to his car to tell him goodnight and we were discussing the "drama" that surrounded us. He slammed his fist on the hood of his car and said, "We'll just get married and see how they like that!"

I was taken by surprise and I laughed at him. He took me in his arms and said, "No, I'm serious." I was trying to be the voice of reason. I reminded him that he was only 17 years old and still in high school. He would never get his mother's permission to marry me.

He said he would. I was so sure his mother would never let him marry me that I told him, "If your Momma says you can marry me, I will marry you." He said okay, and assured me he was on his way home to talk to her right then and he would call me in a little while.

I said a prayer for him as he drove away. Poor Bubba, he was setting himself up for a big let down. I knew his mother. She was one of the most holy women I had ever met. She had a faithful prayer life and she loved everyone unconditionally. I wasn't sure I would be on her list to love after tonight. I knew she wasn't going to say yes but I wanted him to know I would wait on him forever if it took that long to get permission.

About an hour later, he called. She had said no, and in his frustration he had threatened to contact his father who lived in East Texas to get his permission. Bubba's parents had been divorced since he was seven years old. She told him not to do it but he planned on calling his dad first thing in the morning.

I told him not to worry about it. We would be together after he graduated and I wasn't going anywhere. I hung up the phone feeling disappointed but I whispered, "I told you so," just before I went off to sleep.

The next morning my phone rang and his voice made my heart sink. He sounded so awake. He said, "You ready to get married?" My answer, "Sure. When your Momma says you can".

"Ok, she said we can."

"What? You said last night that she said no."

I never expected what came next. "She came in this morning and woke me up. She said she had been praying all night and God gave her a peace about it." I knew if Ann Kennedy said she had peace about it then it was going to be alright. I didn't know what to think. Was I really going to do this?

I knew I loved him more than anything. I knew he was the one I had seen in my dream. I knew I had enough heartache to last a lifetime and it was time for me to be selfish and think of me. I answered, "When do you want to do this?"

He explained that his mother asked if we would give her at least two weeks because she wanted us to have a wedding. A wedding? How was I ever going to afford a wedding? Oh, wait. I need to talk to my momma. Oh, yea. I need to talk to my dad. It was all becoming real now.

The next two weeks flew by. People were really talking about us now. Everyone wondered if we were moving so fast that now we "had" to be married because I had gotten pregnant. Everyone thought we needed counseling because he was too young and we hadn't dated long enough. But no one could convince us to wait. We were determined.

The night before the wedding, it was late and the phone rang. Momma called out to me that Jill was on the phone. I hadn't talked to her since the meeting. I said, "Hello." She said, "Are you ok?" I said, "I'm okay, are you?" She said, "We're okay. I wanted to talk to you before tomorrow. I want you to know that I think you are making a huge mistake. You haven't had time to heal and you are just trying to find some way not to be alone. Bubba is too young and you are both not ready."

I listened quietly to what she had to say as she continued. "Judy, there will never be a man who will put his arms around you and love you like Jesus." She began to cry and so did I. "You will always be looking for someone to make you feel loved and until you find that in Jesus, you are not ready to be married."

Bubba and I had spent hours talking about how we were going to give our lives fully over to God and live life His way. Bubba had spent some time talking and praying with one of the men at the church and had committed to me that He was going to be a Godly man. We were going to begin our marriage right.

Jill insisted that we hadn't had enough time to really know what we were feeling and she just wanted to ask me to wait a while. I assured her that I knew what I was doing and that we had both committed to doing things right. She told me that she loved me and we said goodbye.

Our wedding was "awkward." We were the only ones there who believed we would ever make it more than a few months. His family sat in disbelief as they watched a child of seventeen pledge to love honor and cherish a twenty year old they knew very little about. There were tears, but they were not tears of joy. Well, except for Bubba and me. We cried through the entire ceremony. We were sick in love.

After we were married, things were sweet for a few months and then Bubba began to change. He had lived with his mother all of his life in a home filled with legalism and control. He had rules that were stricter than any I had ever known. No television, no secular music, no shorts etc. His mother was full of love but she felt she was protecting him from sin by shutting out the world.

He began to realize that he was a married man now and that meant he could make his own decisions. During high school, he had used drugs and drank some, hiding it all from his mother. Or so he thought. When we decided to get married, he promised me he would never do that again. Knowing what I had grown up with, it was a deal breaker. I would not live like that in my own home.

His friends at work began using drugs on the job and he got involved with them. He began going out with them to concerts and clubs. I would not compromise on my commitment to God. I insisted he attend church with me even if he wasn't living right. He kept up appearances but we both knew he wasn't making good choices.

There were nights he would come in covered in the smell of drugs. He would lie down beside me and I would grieve as I placed my hand on his shoulder and asked God to save him from himself. I thanked God for bringing him home safe. I was still so over-whelmingly in love with him.

We received the news that I was going to have a baby. Something we should have been excited about. He had maintained from the beginning he wasn't ready for us to have kids just yet. It was an unplanned pregnancy but I wanted him to be happy. He was not.

At first, he was angry. How could I let this happen? He wasn't sure we were going to make it. Knowing all he did about Matthew, he was finding it difficult to trust me. The lifestyle he was living was making him feel extreme guilt and his emotions were becoming too much for him to sort through.

He began to drink and party more heavily and I watched him spiral into a world of addiction I was all too familiar with. During this time, a friend of mine from high school worked at Bubba's job as a secretary. She knew he was my husband and so from time to time when I would call, she and I would tease about him.

I called to talk to him one day and she answered the phone. She said he had left work early and then she asked if she could talk with me a minute. I listened intently as she began to share a con-cern she had. There was a new girl at work and she had let it be known that she was very interested in Bubba. She said she didn't care if he was married.

I asked her if Bubba had been with her, and she answered, "I don't know. Everybody's talking." Then she said, "I think he's with her right now." I thanked her for telling me and I immediately called my home phone. He answered. I said "Hey, what are you doing home so early?" His answer: "I just needed some time off." I acted like I was okay with that and I needed to get back to work so I had to go.

I asked my boss if I could leave because I wasn't feeling well. I drove as fast as I could to get home but he was gone by the time

I got there. I spent the afternoon wondering what I was going to do. I was eight months pregnant, physically sick, emotionally destroyed, and I didn't know how to deal with it.

I got out a suitcase and packed some clothes, just enough for a night or two. I just couldn't decide where to go. I had not shared with anyone how Bubba was acting. I didn't want his mother to be brokenhearted and I didn't want my family to say I told you so.

I had separated myself from most of my friends and family and simply filled my life with only Bubba. Now he had failed me. Once again I found myself facing God and asking, "Why? How much can one person endure in life? How much can my mind take before I lose it? What am I going to do now?"

I sat in silence for what seemed like forever. I put my bag in the closet and waited for him to come home. When he did, I confronted him. My first words to him were, "Who is Carrie?" He looked at me, stunned. "What?" I repeated my question, "Who is Carrie?" He said, "I don't know what you're talking about."

I got up from where I was sitting, walked over to the closet, and pulled out my suitcase. I looked at him and said, "You can tell me who she is or I can leave, it's your choice." He took a deep breath, sighed real heavy then sat down across from me. "Okay. Okay, I'll tell you. She's a girl from work I been messing around with."

"Did you sleep with her?" A heavy silence filled the room. He didn't want to answer and I didn't want to hear the answer. "Yes." I stood up slow, walked across the room, and picked up my bag. I didn't know what else to do. He reached and took the bag from me and asked me to at least talk it over.

He explained that he had been running around with some of the guys at work and they brought her and some other girls along for fun. They would all do drugs and get drunk together. It just happened.

He promised he would stop doing that and he would tell her he's not interested at all. He would tell her that he loves his wife and doesn't want to lose her, if I would just give him one more chance. I asked if this was the first time and if she was the only one.

I asked for her phone number. He asked me to let him call her. I agreed as long as I was there listening when he called her. I asked him to make the call right then and I stood around the corner in the hall while he called. He told her his wife knew what had happened and he just wanted her to know he didn't want anything else to happen.

We spent the next few hours discussing all of the things he had done that were wrong and I felt my heart being ripped out of my chest one sliver at a time. I had been here before. I was well acquainted with the damage a man can do. My heart was asking the same question again, Why can't I just die?

This time it was different. I couldn't. I had a life inside of me waiting to live. I had to pull myself together and make this work. I went through a grieving process for the next several weeks. I could barely stand to feel him touch me. My mind would immediately begin playing pictures of him with someone else; it was like open heart surgery with no anesthetic.

He was so ashamed of himself. I could see the pain it was causing him to watch me suffer so. He truly loved me and the consequences of his choices were overwhelming. I believed him. I just couldn't forgive him fully right then. I wanted to. I wanted to forget, but my emotions were ravaged. I was totally alone in my brokenness once again. I had no one to turn to but God.

August 28, 1983

Oh my God. I am hurting, no I am dying. This time I'm done. How could this happen? How could he love me and hurt me? How could he betray me after all I've come through? Now this?

The one I trusted with my heart. The one I trusted to protect me has stabbed me right through the heart and I don't know how to heal.

I hear you say you understand. I hear you say you were betrayed too. It still doesn't seem real to me. I want to forgive him. I just can't yet.

Oh my God, I deserve this. Is this my punishment for all those years of lies? How can I feel sorry for myself when I am only experiencing what Jill must have felt? I'm sick, God. I'm sick.

Please help me! I can't go on but I have to. This baby needs me to be strong right now but I am falling fast.

Oh God.

APPLICATION

Marriage is a God-creation. It is a very good thing. When given proper care and attention, it is the strongest bond of two human hearts. Left unprotected, it can be one of the most devastating, heart-wrenching experiences.

Only the strong survive they say. I guess I beat the odds. Bubba and I have now been married for over twenty-eight years. Today, we are strong but the journey had a lot of winding roads. I am determined to continue to guard my marriage as something sacred and life-sustaining.

It takes two to make it work and two to make it fail. I've been counseling with couples for several years and I've discovered there are always three sides to every situation. His side, her side, and the truth. All three are vitally important to the restoration process.

I've also discovered a basic fact of relationship. When two people are fully committed to God it is much easier for those same two people to remain fully committed to each other. The common denominator of faith has without fail, been the determining factor in restored lives and marriages. With faith, there is always room for each person to give more. When your wants, needs, and desires become more important to me than my wants, needs, and desires, we are then ready to have a successful relationship.

Marriage has become an exchange business. If I don't like the spouse I have, I'll simply exchange them for someone else. It's just easier to give up and move on. The challenge with this kind of thinking is that we are the same person moving on to a different person who will inevitably lead us back to the same problem.

This cycle will repeat itself until the emotional damage in our hearts is totally irreparable. Along with the breakdown of trust in relationships, there are usually a few children caught in the middle of the exchange process.

These children grow up believing that it is normal to simply to give up when it gets too hard. Generations of broken families can be affected by one marriage. One couple who will stand and fight for a good marriage can change the effects of brokenness for a lifetime to follow.

Obviously, God's hand was at work in my marriage. I've learned again that pain is my greatest teacher. I've learned by experience that true love is this—when we are willing to lay down our lives for another.

As I travel and minister, I have seen the devastation of broken marriages. I know that God can restore broken trust because I have experienced it. The fact that I have lived through it offers hope to all who are in the middle of it.

I have come to a greater understanding of the love of God. The kind of love that says, "I know you have failed me, but I loved you while you were involved in sin." The kind of love that says, "Even if it kills me to love you, I will." It's God's kind of love that chooses to love me, "while I am still sinning."

God was not absent when I was hurting. I was not alone; He was holding me and crying with me. He is moved by my heartache. He loved Bubba as much as he loved me and wanted to help us both. He taught me to teach others that forgiveness is difficult but it's always worth it. By the way, Matthew and Jill are still married today. God does miracles.

He heals the brokenhearted.
Psalm 147:3

DEATH BY DESIGN

Insert: From "Who Washed the Sky?"

CIRCUMSTANCE

The cold November air brushed across my face as I stared across the horizon of statues and people. I could not be more exhausted physically or emotionally. Recent days had been filled with hectic preparation for a ceremonial event, the sacred memorial service. I was seated alone for a brief moment, trying to make my thoughts come together so that I could discern the delay.

Why were we waiting so long to begin the final moments of this heart-wrenching experience and where were my mom and dad? I felt more alone in that moment than any I could remember. I saw my husband seated in one of the white folding chairs and surrounded there by his concerned family. They had walked through this ordeal with us and were trying to cover their emotions while struggling to comfort him.

I looked at the tiny blue casket as my mind raced back a day or so to the moment I first saw it at the funeral home. How could I possibly walk through that room of death boxes and select one appropriate for my only begotten son. How could I be expected to reasonably distinguish the best color for his final resting crib?

I chose blue because it seemed manly. I thought his blue eyes and blond hair would coordinate with the background and I didn't want it to be just a box. I knew we didn't have the finances to cover all of the mounting expenses related to his illness, and now his death, but I had no choice. I was not going to look back someday and remember that I had buried my son in the least expensive box available.

I was summoned back to reality as a loving, slender arm slipped around my shoulder and hovered to block the wind from my face, now wet with tears. I recognized her voice as she whispered, "I love you. I'm so, so sorry." It was Brenda, my faithful, undeserved friend of a lifetime. She must have noticed I was sitting alone and could not bear to watch.

I let her know that we were waiting for my parents. They must have gotten lost somewhere between the church and the grave-side. I hated to begin the internment without them, but it was so cold and everyone had been waiting a long time. Brenda's presence beside me was comforting. I hadn't realized how cold and alone I was feeling until the sincerity of her words soothed my mind, even if for a moment. Oh, thank you God, for placing such a graceful friend in my life.

Just four days before, I had received a call from her checking in to see if I was okay, and asking how I was dealing with things. It was the morning we were to check Zack into the hospital. He was to have a heart catheterization the following morning to relieve pressure from his heart.

I can remember the conversation well. I said to her, "It's like you know the inevitable is going to happen, you feel like you're in slow motion and there's nothing you can do to stop it." Again, she said, "I'm so sorry." I was sincerely afraid, but I wanted to ensure everyone that I had great faith. With her, I could simply be honest. "I'm scared and I don't know if I can do this."

At the age of twenty-three, nothing could have prepared me to handle the days ahead. We said our goodbyes after I promised to keep her updated on the situation and I finished packing for the trip to the hospital. We checked into the sixth floor of Children's Medical Center, Dallas. We were not first timers. The familiar red wagons and treatment rooms were sights we had become accustomed to.

The sixth floor was the heart center. We had first visited thirteen months before to receive our terminal diagnosis. Dr. David Fixler was such a quiet-spoken gentleman. I'm sure it was extremely difficult for him to sit across the desk from what appeared to be two children and offer us the desperate news that our son had a very serious congenital heart disorder. The name he gave it was "Aortic atresia and hyperplasia left heart."

At that moment, he could have said, "bla bla bla…." and it would have made as much sense to us. He took out a small piece of paper and began to draw a diagram of a heart chamber. As he detailed the specific problem areas, we continued to believe he was preparing to offer us an answer. A treatment or a surgery to repair the disorder, but he finished his explanations with a negative head shake. Left to right, right to left and then back to center.

I broke the silence with a simple response. "Are you saying we can't afford the surgery, or you won't perform it?" His answer came swiftly and softly, "Oh no, I'm saying there is no surgery that will fix it." The room was quiet, I looked at Bubba, he looked at me, and then we looked back at the doctor. "Not even a heart transplant?"

"Zack's heart deformity is complicated by the fact that he does not have a functioning valve to connect another heart to." "Can't you guys make one? I know I've heard of plastic valves?" "Only God could make something that complicated."

"So what do we do now? How long will he live like this?" Again, his calm, tranquil demeanor, "Not long. We will try to make him as comfortable as possible, but we don't expect him to survive more than a week or two."

"I'm so sorry." Those words, those three words. So final, so hard to say and harder still to receive. The next few days were spent in the hospital room waiting. How is a mother, so young and inexperienced, supposed to hold her precious child in her arms and wait for him to stop breathing?

The waiting was complicated by the issue of illness in my own body. I hadn't recovered physically from the emergency c-section just a week and a half before. I was hemorrhaging and growing weak. I had been instructed to stay in bed for two more weeks because I wasn't recovering well. There was no way I was going to leave my baby's side knowing his prognosis. So devastated and exhausted, I chose to stay.

The machines he wasconnected to were intended to alarm us the moment he stopped breathing. False alarms would scream out, throwing my heart into a panicked frenzy of overwhelming anguish. It felt like a never-ending cruel experiment of faith verses sanity.

Two weeks later, the social worker for the hospital came into our room to meet with us. We had no insurance whatsoever. We were very young and still living on love. But trust me, all the love we had could not pay the mountain of charges that were adding up. It was time for us to take our son home and wait there for him to die.

We made the best of a difficult situation. We moved him home into his own room and made preparations to care for him there. We brought in the machines and we were determined to learn the steps for his care. Following several more nights of false "death" alarms, we finally made the choice to remove the monitors and trust God. Okay. If he is going to die, it will be silently and peacefully.

We were to take him in for check-ups every two weeks, if he was still living. The doctors were amazed that he continued to grow and develop at the same rate of other children his age. It wasn't long until he began to call out syllables and sound out the words "Momma" and "Dada." Our hearts would thrill at every new venture. He would toddle around in his walker and make joyful sounds that delighted his young parents.

Often there were moments when we would forget his illness and allow ourselves to daydream, to temporarily imagine what he would be like as a young man. He would certainly be a talented musician and singer. It's in the family. He would surely succeed in sports. It's in the family. He would grow to love God and most appropriately serve in some ministry. It's in the family.

Of course the doctors were astonished at his progress but maintained their diagnosis to be correct. Eventually, his heart would get too tired and simply stop beating. Around six months of age, he did begin to show a few signs of weakening. If he cried for any length of time, he would begin to throw up whatever food he was able to take in. His weakness made it difficult for him to eat very much at a time.

The discomfort affected his ability to sleep for long periods of time. His entire life, he never slept more than two hours at a time. This made for very long nights. Ann, Bubba's mother, and Kathy, his sister, moved into our tiny apartment to help with his care. They would take the night shifts and I would handle the days.

We carried him everywhere on a special pillow and never allowed him to cry for anything. We found a way to make him comfortable so that he would not get exhausted. We knew it was imperative that he hold his food down for strength.

Around the time he was about nine months old, we began to notice that his color was slipping. The blue around his mouth was becoming more noticeable and he didn't seem as happy as he had in recent months. We loved watching him make his way around the coffee table and then simply rest his head for a while. But then he would begin to cry for what appeared to be no reason. We know now that it was pressure building up in his heart and causing headaches.

The doctors remained puzzled. They had not seen a child with this rare condition ever live past two weeks. They brought in specialist from England to study his case. Each specialist would come back with the same diagnosis, "He is terminal, we just don't know when."

As people of faith, our choice was to believe that God was somehow prolonging his life to perform a great miracle for us. We had so many friends and family members praying continually. We knew more ministers than most people because of our history in traveling and ministry. Every person we knew who could speak the name of God was praying for our son.

It was finally time to celebrate his first birthday! What a day. Our church allowed us to use the gym facilities located adjacent to the church. It was a huge room, full of echoes, and I can remember the smell was unusual. It was possibly the mix of wet towels and over-used basketballs. We were simply thankful that it had been offered to us for free and it was large enough to host all of our friends and family.

Mom was so sensitive to how we were feeling. She wasn't able to care for Zack because it required special training and so she did everything she could to help financially and spiritually. That day, she had hired a group of clowns to come in and entertain all of us. They were amazing with balloons and Zach's eyes were full of wonder as he watched them move hats and noses. Mom had worked extra hours to pay for this special gift and she insisted it was so worth it. It was amazing.

The gifts he received were indescribable. At the age of one, he received his first bicycle. It was as if all of his friends and family wanted to give him everything they could just in case he didn't make it to the next birthday. What an experience.

There we were celebrating his life on his birthday, October 8th, realizing it was time to return to his heart specialist for another check up. We had established relationships with some of the nurses in the heart clinic and were encouraged because they knew what we were going through. This time, Dr. Fixler decided that Zack was becoming increasingly uncomfortable because of the huge amount of pressure building up in his heart.

His suggestion was to take him in and perform what he called a minor surgical procedure. A heart catheterization. They would insert a small wire like tube into his leg and feed it up into his heart. When they got to his heart they would be able to open a small underdeveloped valve and release some of the pressure. The description of the procedure sounded barbaric to me but I realized we had to do something soon. Zack was hurting and becoming much weaker.

Obviously, Dr. Fixler advised us of the risks involved and we completely understood that in Zack's case, this procedure could very well be fatal. His heart was not strong enough to take much more but he was so uncomfortable and in so much pain it would be impossible for him to continue without some type of intervention.

That decision was challenging. We loved our little "Sunshine Boy." He was everything to us. But we lived with him every day and could clearly see that he was in a huge amount of pain. It would have been selfish for us to choose to allow him to continue to suffer when we were being offered the possibility of relieving the pressure and helping him find an escape from the pain.

However, the fear of losing our most prized possession in the entire world was overwhelming. How could we make this decision? It was possible that he would make it through and the procedure could possibly buy a little more time. Without it, he would continue to grow increasingly uncomfortable and unless God did our miracle, eventually his heart would give in from exhaustion.

The anxiety overwhelmed us. Wasn't there someone else who could make this decision for us? Our friends and family who tried to support us through it all could not offer any advice. They feared to counsel either way, considering the risk involved. Who can blame them? I wouldn't want to be the one who said, "Go for it" or "Don't" in the event of death.

Finally, we simply decided to try to make our son more comfortable. His pain was reaching levels we could no longer control. He wasn't holding down food well at all and we could not bear to watch him suffer like that. So with the decision made, the date was set—November 21, 1984. It would be the day after our third wedding anniversary.

After checking in and completing all of the forms necessary for surgery, we were assigned a sixth floor room and settled in. We asked our family if we could have that night with Zack alone. Usually, Ann and Kathy would try to stay to relieve us for sleep but we simply wanted to be with him as Momma and Dada.

They chose to stay, but honored our request by staying in the waiting room. Their kindness and loving support was beyond description. We could not have survived without their constant love and care for Zack. He belonged to all of us.

Just down the hall from his room was the playroom, a beautifully decorated room with everything bright and fun that a kid would want to play with. We took turns pulling him around in the little red wagon and taking trips down to the playroom. I suggested that Bubba get some sleep while I played with him and then we could switch.

My shift was first and I remember moments of that night very clearly. We found ourselves over by the window looking out at the bright night lights. I asked, "Can you see the lights?" He pointed at the window and said, "Lights?" I thought about lights and how they lit up darkness. My eyes filled with tears but I didn't want him to sense my heartache so I began to sing.

I had written a lullaby for Zack when he was just a few days old. I began to sing it to him and watched as he relaxed for a minute and looked right into my eyes. He placed his hands on my face and kissed my nose. My heart began to swell with joy at that intimate moment I was given to share with my "Sunshine Boy." He was my light and I could not begin to imagine life without him.

I spent the next few hours cherishing his every move as if I knew it was my last moment with him on this earth. No, I did not know for sure. I wanted him to live more than anyone did, I just didn't know what would happen and I wasn't going to waste my sacred last hours with him questioning God's sovereignty.

Time passed quickly and before I knew it, Bubba was at the door of the playroom and wanted his time with his son. I went back to the room and tried to rest but sleep would not come. I simply rocked in the chair and waited for the sun to come up.

When Bubba and Zack returned to the room, we took the wagon ride down the hall to the waiting area and woke up Ann and Kathy. There we sat and prayed for a moment. I remember whispering, "God, please give me back my son today. Please?" Ann and Kathy faithfully declared God's healing and Bubba wept softly. Some moments are locked in your heart. I remember the smell of Zach's head as we held him while we prayed. That cannot be taken from me.

The nurses came to take the long walk down the hall with us and when we arrived at the elevators that led to the surgical wing, they showed us to the waiting area and assured us they would come out and get us once the procedure was completed.

Time was silent. All I could hear in the waiting area was the rhythmic breathing of our family as our hearts pounded in our chests. The urgency of the moment made the clock seem broken. I know we were all in a constant attitude of prayer, but none of us chose to speak out loud. The silence was interrupted by a familiar call, "Code blue in O-R 2." The call system pierced through the silence and shook me from my chair. My heart jumped and fear gripped me. I slipped out into the hall, found a phone, and called Brenda. Once again, I reached out to the one I knew I could lean on.

"I'm scared. There's something wrong. All of these people are running toward the door and I don't know what is going on." She simply said, "I'm on my way." At that point, one of the nurses appeared at the doorway and waved us over to a different waiting room. She was very business-like and obviously well trained to handle these delicate situations.

We walked in with mixed emotions. "The doctor will be in to speak with you in just a moment." Her tone and her countenance were reverent and rehearsed. I sat by the door and Bubba leaned against the wall. Everyone else gathered in around the room as the doctor made his way inside and closed the door behind him.

His words soft and quiet again, a little shaky this time, "We did all that we could do. I'm so sorry, we lost him." What? What did he say? We lost him? As shock moved around the room, Bubba crumbled to the ground and I leaned over to catch my breath. As quickly as he had fallen, he stood and with determination I heard him demand, "Where is he? I want to see him now!"

I knew he was in shock and the doctor realized nothing would stop him. He assured him that he could go in with him in just a few moments as soon as they had completed preparing him. It was a moment of pandemonium, everyone was weeping, shaking, and grieving and there I stood with no words. I had no words. I could not make a sound. I could feel the hot tears pouring from my eyes, but I had no words.

They came in to lead Bubba into the operating room where Zack was lying. He was wrapped in a white sheet and the tubes had all been removed. His face and hands had been washed with a baby scented wash and his hair had been combed. I waited for few moments then walked over to the door of the operating room. It was dark and I felt a chill as I entered the doorway. Father and son were sitting over beside the table cuddled together in a peaceful moment of anguish. He was quietly singing to him and motioned for me to come near.

I thought I would fall, my steps were shaky and my eyes were blurred by the tears I could not control. I still had no words. If I made sounds, they were simply grief spilling out as a quiet groaning. We stood there together holding each other. Our sweet little family experienced the sting of death for what felt like hours. Then there was a shadow at the door, Ann wanted to come in and out of honor for her, I slipped out and made my way alone down the long corridor.

I recognized the slender figure of a quiet blonde friend walking toward me. It was Brenda, coming to my rescue again. She must have been so challenged for words. Until now, she had always been the one I could count on for true sound advice, but at the moment we were both overwhelmed with heartache. I fell into her arms for a brief moment and then something strange happened. It was as though my mind "clicked." I said, "I have to go gather his things from his room." I stopped crying and walked very deliberately to the elevator and pushed the number six. I moved with intention and focus directly down the hall to his room and began to pack his things into his little balloon-covered bag.

All of the exhausting emotions of the day had shut down. It was like someone reached into my heart and turned it off. I could not feel. After a few moments, Bubba appeared at the door with our pastor and they came in for prayer. We stood there as we heard sincere words of concern and comfort but I continued to feel nothing more. Emotion was absent.

We made the long drive home, knowing what would be facing us there. The climb up the stairs to the apartment seemed like Mount Everest and as I walked into his room, briefly, like waves, emotion returned. I felt as though God had distanced Himself from me and I was alone in an empty room of heart-wrenching sorrow. Bubba could not come in. He was having great difficulty processing it all and had simply collapsed on the couch.

Precious Bubba. He was barely twenty years old and in no mental shape to know how to handle this kind of heartache. He loved God. He loved his wife. He loved his son. He just did not have the emotional ability to function in this blurry darkness. I sat down beside him to explain how we needed to make arrangements for the funeral service. It was only a few days before Thanksgiving and the funeral home needed us to finalize the plans as soon as possible.

He stared forward for a few moments and then turned to me and whispered, "I can't do it." I knew he couldn't do it. I also knew that meant that I would. One of us was going to make the decisions and he was in no shape to function. He barely uttered a word for the next few days. My heart was hurting for him but I could do nothing more than function in fulfilling the requirements of making arrangements for our "Sunshine Boy."

Once again, all emotion left my body and I began to function like a robot. I made the trip to the funeral home and selected a burial plot in "Baby Land" at Restland Memorial Park. They said it was beautiful and a special place where all of the babies were together. They showed me a statue of Jesus and a beautiful tree nearby. I nodded that it would be a fine selection and we moved on to caskets and clothing.

I don't know how I would have handled making all of those detailed decisions if it had not been for my sweet mother and my brother-in-law, Randall, who was good at handling business deals. The dollar figures alone caused my mind to ache. I had no idea the kind of finances required to pay for all of these expenses. Step by step, we finalized all of the plans. I was exhausted and cold as we drove back home that evening.

It was a Wednesday. We usually tried to attend church on Wednesdays but that was certainly not in the plans this evening. Our pastor did call to check in on us and verify that we had completed the service plans. In an unusually awkward moment, he asked if I would share with him the total cost of the arrangements. I quickly listed a few of the numbers and he hurried off the phone. It was almost time for church service to begin so I didn't find his actions strange.

Later that evening, I was trying to get Bubba to eat something when the doorbell rang. It was the pastor and one of the Bible teachers from our church. I assumed they had come to check on Bubba. By this time the news of Zack's death and the devastation it was having on Bubba was distressing everyone. They sat down beside him and offered comforting words. They took both of our hands and prayed with us. I'm sure they had no idea what words would have been appropriate to minister comfort to two children who had just lost a child.

Just before they left for the evening, they handed us an envelope that contained the amount owed to the funeral home. We both began to cry as we realized our church family had raised the funds to help us when we could not help ourselves. Over and over again, the words would sound, "I'm so sorry. I wish we could do more."

That November had to be one of the coldest on record. Sitting there beside Brenda, I realized that I was actually going to have to get up and move on with my life. Isn't that how it is? We really don't get a choice. "The Lord giveth and the Lord taketh away." As long as we live, those we love will die.

Mom and Dad arrived and we moved on with the internment and prayer. I held onto my daddy for a while afterwards. I could tell his heart was broken for me. It really bothered him that they had gotten lost and had arrived late. It wasn't an issue with me, he was there in that moment and I was thankful. I felt so small in his arms, I felt safe and I wanted him to take me home and protect me from this horrible pain I was beginning to feel.

I looked around for Bubba; maybe he could take me home and make this feel better. There he was surrounded again by so many. I couldn't get to him. He called out for me and they made way for me to be seated beside him. I understood at that moment, we would go on. I wasn't sure how, but we would.

Several months passed as we struggled to find the will to continue on. It is our faith that established our survival. Long hours spent sharing memories seasoned by grief drew us closer together than ever before. We both recommitted our lives whole heartedly to God and His service and we trusted Him to sustain us.

A few months after Zack's death, we made the decision to attend a different church. It was an amazing change. Bubba really began to grow in His spiritual walk. I had not seen this type of spiritual hunger in him before. I could not understand the pace of his development and the depth of his determination to follow hard after God.

He would spend days fasting and praying. So many nights he would kiss me goodnight and slip into the back room of our home for time with God. He had developed quite a prayer life. He is a quiet man by nature, but when he prays, the walls shake. I had never known anyone to fast as much and as often so I became concerned. I asked our new pastor about it but he assured me it was good for him.

A few months later, we accepted the position of youth leaders and Bubba continued to develop his spiritual stamina. Those days were filled with activity and life as we began to learn the ups and downs of ministry. It's been over 30 years now and I can say with confidence, he has become the most devoted husband, loving father, honorable pastor, and sincerely dedicated Christian I have ever known. Thank you God for life-altering power!

November 24, 1984

I cannot take anymore. I know I've been told that God will not give us more than we can bear. But, I'm quite sure right now – this is it. My mind cannot comprehend why. I know I've never been perfect but do I deserve this much heartache? I'm not supposed to be angry at God, but right now – I just don't know what I feel.

What are you doing God? Am I supposed to trust you here? Are you going to do a miracle for me now? I know it is appointed unto "man" once to die but God; my son is not a man…. He's just a baby. Why now?

Dealing with the land of the living when you are walking through the Valley of the Shadow of death can be one of the most difficult things you can do. The process of grieving the loss of a child is unlike any other form of grief. The death of a child violates the natural order of things. Old people die, children do not–right?

My world revolved around my son. Most mothers' lives are filled with the care and nurture of their children. The inescapable heaviness of heartache is difficult to put into words and often totally misunderstood. Psychotherapists are considering placing a new category in the medical books.

Child-loss grief is so traumatic that our lives become quite debilitated as a result. The healing process is an extensive work of healing that can take years. Coping with the death of a child is the biggest burden any parent could possibly bear. It is necessary to develop a support network to help walk with you through this difficult season.

Experts say that parents typically never get over the loss of a child, but rather learn to adjust. One-third of parents who lose a child report that their marriage suffers and oftentimes fails. It is vital that a couple who has suffered the loss of a child share their pain. Don't try to go through this alone. Communication and counseling can make a huge difference in adjusting to life after death.

Avoid isolation. Often, friends and family do not know how to handle the situation and choose to avoid those who are grieving. They don't know what to say and are fearful of saying or doing the wrong thing. Remind them how much you need their support at this time, even if it is in silence.

The devastation of losing my son cannot completely be described using words. So many have asked how I could know that God was actually working to bring life through death.

My husband and I have had some long discussions regarding the question of God's sovereignty in the matter. He is convinced if it had not been for the sickness and eventual death of our son, he may never have had his spiritual life restored.

I maintain that God would not punish me to fix my husband's life. But really, who am I? God's ways are not mine. His plans and thoughts are so high above mine, they exceed understanding.

I truly believe God knew ahead of time ultimately what would come of Zack's death. He knew the lives that would be affected and He saw down through the years that would follow to see the countless number of broken mothers I would be able to reach.

People can offer comfort to us when we are dealing with broken hearts. People can bring food to our homes and send flowers. Sympathy cards say really nice things and scriptures offering peace make a difference. But the voice I will hear when I am ravaged by the death of my child is the voice of another mother who has stood where I stand.

God has allowed me opportunities to walk into doors that would have never been opened if I had not experienced the desolation of death. I can hold the hand of a mother whose child is heading for surgery and assure her that our God will be in control of that operating room.

I can encourage those who are struggling with grief recovery that the light will shine again, and with God's help they can go on. When you have lived it, you can explain it. When you have felt it, you can understand it. It's empathy, not sympathy.

God's promise to be close to the brokenhearted is true. He has always drawn close to me when I felt I couldn't face another day. I can sense His presence so strong when I walk through a children's hospital and see room after room filled with fear though the Prince of Peace is walking the halls.

I will not allow the sting of death to silence the voice of my Peace Speaker. He will turn this for my good. He alone knows what I can bear.

We do not know what we can survive. Only God knows the plans He has for us. I have been determined to use Zack's death for the Glory of God, to use his story to display the restoration process God has used in my life.

Only in heaven, will we fully discover what fourteen months on earth accomplished for eternity. God so loved the world, that He gave His only begotten Son, that whosoever believeth on Him should not perish but have everlasting life! Because He gave His only begotten Son, I will see my only begotten son again!

Brandon Zachary Kennedy

October 8,1983 – November 21,1984

"God's Got a Hand in It"

My life has not been easy. God never promised it would be. Actually, He said, "When you pass through the water, I will be with you and the rivers will not overflow you; when you walk through the fire, you will not be burned…" Obviously He knew I would be walking through some things.

There were days I believed I would never make it through. There were times I wondered where He was. There were also days when I knew I had failed so miserably. The heaviness of shame caused me to want to hide from Him.

His plan was for me to know fullness in life and to experience the good plans He had for me. He was not taken by surprise by my circumstances. He was never shocked at the places He found me. He always knew where I was.

I choose to believe the entire Bible. If all of my days were numbered and decided before I was born, then He wants me to be aware of His watchful eye from the moment I drew my first breath. He knew me completely; He was there when I was being formed in my mother's womb. I have to believe He was not looking the other way during the seasons of life that brought such heartache.

Consider this—God is good. He cannot be any other way. He is innately good. He cannot be bad. His actions toward me are only for my good.

God did not accidentally lose me the days I was being abused. He didn't forget to deliver me out of danger when I fell into danger. He wasn't teasing with me when my heart was continually crushed by life.

He allowed me to choose. He made provision to rescue and redeem my life. The unspeakable things I experienced have now been used to speak of His redeeming power. The world deemed me a statistic of an alcoholic home. He re-deemed me to be a child of the King. Circumstances deemed me poor and broken, He re-deemed me to be fully satisfied in everything. Men in my life had deemed me used merchandise. He re-deemed me to be a brand new creature in Christ Jesus.

Mom went to heaven in December of 2006. I was my dad's caregiver for the five years that followed. He made every effort to have the hard conversations with us, eventually asking us to forgive the years he had wasted. He accepted Christ as his personal Savior three months before he died. I had forgiven him many years before he asked.

All of the "crap" that I have experienced has been considered, weighed, and checked by God's hand. He knew the lives that would be affected by the truth of His purposes. He saw all of my weaknesses and failures and He determined that they would be the very things that would demonstrate His strength in my life.

God is fully aware of what was, what is, and what will be. I can rest easy and trust Him with all of the rest of my days. I've been through enough to know He'll be enough for me.

Romans 3:21-24 MSG

"...Out of sheer generosity he put us in right standing with himself. A pure gift. He got us out of the mess we're in and restored us to where He always wanted us to be. ..."

ABOUT THE AUTHOR

Judy Kennedy serves as Co-Pastor of Mustang Creek Community Church in Forney, TX. She and her husband Robert have spent 34 of their 37 years of marriage in ministry. A gifted communicator, Judy's credibility comes from her life experiences. An amazing testimony of God's faithfulness and a true example of overcoming power; her life is full of truth lived out. Her history includes perseverance through devastating challenges which she insists developed in her God's purpose. Growing up in a seriously dysfunctional home, experiencing abuse in difficult relationships, suffering the loss of a child, and enduring complicated health issues, she has discovered God's ability to take the difficult things in life and use them for His glory. Along with an anointed international speaking ministry, Judy is an exceptional writer. Judy currently offers parenting and marriage enrichment advice as a columnist, "Just Judy." She enjoys blogging, vlogging, and writing for a local magazine. She has authored four books: *Holy Crap, Who Washed the Sky, It's Just Judy,* and *Chasing Legacy.* Judy's simple presentation of truth is covered with a passionate anointing and an abundant amount of joy. It's been said, "If a merry heart does good like a medicine—Judy is God's prescription!

Contact Info:

JudyKennedy.net 469-358-6921

Mustang Creek Community Church
13851 FM 548
Forney, TX 75126